THE
JAPANESE
AMERICAN
EXPERIENCE

Minorities in Modern America

Editors
Warren F. Kimball
David Edwin Harrell, Jr.

THE JAPANESE AMERICAN EXPERIENCE

DAVID J. O'BRIEN
AND
STEPHEN S. FUGITA

INDIANA
UNIVERSITY
PRESS
BLOOMINGTON
AND
INDIANAPOLIS

The paper used in this publication meets the minimum requirements of American National Standard for Information Sciences—Permanence of Paper for Printed Library Materials, ANSI Z39.48-1984.

♾™

Manufactured in the United States of America

Library of Congress Cataloging-in-Publication Data

O'Brien, David J.
　The Japanese American experience / David J. O'Brien and Stephen S. Fujita
　　p.　cm.—(Minorities in modern America)
　Includes bibliographical references and index.
　ISBN 0-253-34164-7 (cloth). — ISBN 0-253-20656-1 (paper)
　1. Japanese Americans—History. I. Fujita, Stephen S., date.
II. Title. III. Series.
E184.J3027　1991
973'. 04956—dc20   90-23961

1 2 3 4 5 95 94 93 92 91

CONTENTS

	Introduction	1
ONE	The Early Years	14
TWO	Portents of the Incarceration	38
THREE	The Concentration Camp Experience	60
FOUR	Postwar Assimilation	83
FIVE	The Persistence of Community	101
SIX	The Future of Japanese Americans	118
	Appendixes	137
	Bibliographic Essay	147
	References	155
	Index	169

Illustrations follow Chapter 2.

THE
JAPANESE
AMERICAN
EXPERIENCE

INTRODUCTION

 What is the popular image of Japanese Americans? Less than fifty years ago persons of Japanese ancestry were seen by many Americans, especially on the West Coast, as incapable of being assimilated into this society. According to the then-current stereotype, they were from such a different culture that they could never adopt American ways. This "logic" was used in the 1910s and 1920s as a rationale for legislation to keep Japanese immigrants from owning land, to prevent them from becoming American citizens, and eventually to stop all immigration from Japan to the United States. Later, it became the justification for the most serious breakdown of constitutional rights in modern American history when Japanese Americans were herded into concentration camps during World War II. Large segments of the public and many government officials presumed that loyalty to Japan would override any identification even American-born Japanese might have with their country. This presumption proved to be singularly incorrect. No Japanese American was ever convicted of committing a single act of espionage or sabotage during the war.

Fortunately, most Americans' impressions of Japanese Americans have changed rather dramatically since the end of World War II. Today, the label Japanese American is more likely to evoke images of "hard work," "strong families," and perhaps "good in math" (Maykovich 1971). By almost any standard, Japanese Americans have been quite successful in achieving a solid middle class standing in American society. They are by and large well educated and overrepresented in the professions, and their mean income is higher than that of white Americans (see chapter 4; appendixes 5, 7, 8, 9; Kan and Liu 1986). Moreover, they appear to be highly

1

assimilated; the vast majority live in predominantly Caucasian neighborhoods, and currently over 50 percent of all new marriages involving Japanese Americans are with Caucasians (Kitano et al. 1984).

Indeed, it is the apparent "success story" of Japanese Americans, especially in comparison with the persistent economic and social problems experienced by some other American racial minorities, that has captured the attention of numerous sociologists (e.g., Peterson 1970). Many—especially younger—Japanese Americans, however, find this type of Horatio Alger characterization offensive and indicative of a subtle racism. Neither the recent stereotype nor the earlier one reflects the complex reality of individual Japanese Americans who, like persons in other ethnic groups, are trying to reconcile the competing demands of tradition and the need to cope with change. Further, this "model minority" image diverts attention from the serious structural problems of inequality which remain in American society.

Successive generations of Japanese Americans have had to deal with strikingly different historical circumstances. The first-generation immigrant Issei were treated as a lower caste minority by the larger society. Their basic struggle was to find ways to make a living within a very limited set of options. The second-generation Nisei grew up knowing they were Americans but experienced second class citizenship. This culminated in the humiliation and economic hardship of the wartime internment. After the war, the Nisei, although still experiencing discrimination in certain settings, had a greater number of occupational opportunities than was ever dreamed of by their parents' generation. The third-generation Sansei face new challenges as they now enter the full spectrum of mainstream occupations. They must somehow reconcile their generally middle-class and relatively discrimination-free childhood and early adulthood with the fact that despite their apparent "100-percent Americanness" they still retain elements of a culture which is markedly different from the dominant European roots of American culture (Miyamoto 1986–87).

Two main themes weave through the Japanese American experience. The first is what sociologists term "structural constraints," which pertain mainly, although not exclusively, to discriminatory actions and pressures that limited the options available to Japanese

Americans and that have produced a set of conditions quite different from those faced by white immigrant groups from Europe. These structural constraints have been a major handicap with which Japanese Americans, along with other "persons of color," have struggled.

The second theme pertains to the responses of Japanese Americans to these structural constraints. Although each of the challenges they faced were unique historical situations that could hardly have been anticipated prior to their arrival in the United States, the kinds of responses made to these exigencies were strongly influenced by Japanese culture. This can be seen especially in their ability to organize collectively to deal with economic, social, and political problems. In this regard, it is clear that the cultural blueprints for organizing people for concerted action, which the Issei brought with them from Japan, gave them a distinct advantage over most of the European immigrant groups which landed in the New World during the nineteenth and early twentieth centuries. These cultural blueprints were not merely vague "values" or "beliefs," but rather specific principles for creating social organizations.

THE LEGACY FROM JAPAN

In subsequent chapters, we will devote considerable attention to the structural constraints which the Japanese immigrants and their children had to face during different periods. At this juncture, however, it is important for the reader to get a sense of the cultural legacy the Japanese immigrants brought with them to America and how that legacy produced a set of principles of collective organization which influenced how they dealt with those problems.

A key element in explaining the Japanese experience in America is the belief which the Issei brought with them to the New World that they were a single people, irrespective of class or region of origin, with a complete culture and clear social boundaries between themselves and other peoples of the world. Indeed, many scholars support the Japanese perception that they are among the most homogeneous people in the world, on both physical and cultural dimensions. A single language, for example, was spoken in Japan for several centuries before the immigrants left for the

New World (Haglund 1984; Nakane 1970, 140–142). As early as the seventh century the Japanese saw themselves as a single people living in a unified nation (Reischauer 1981, 8). By the time of the Meiji restoration in the nineteenth century, the uniqueness of the Japanese people had been formally stated in the Constitution and the Imperial Rescript on Education (Ichioka 1971).

The Japanese historical situation is an example of what Castile terms a "persistent people." He says:

> *The* defining characteristic of a persistent people is a continuity of common identity based, Spicer suggests, on "common understandings concerning the meaning of a set of symbols." . . . The symbols may in fact change, as does all else in the adapting entity, but, as long as a continuity is maintained in the symbol system sufficient to define a collective identity separate from that of surrounding peoples, endurance occurs. [1981, xviii]

The degree of homogeneity and sense of peoplehood found among the Japanese during the nineteenth century is striking. At the same time, the majority of countries in both Europe and Asia were beset by struggles to achieve a sense of national identity in the face of resistance by citizens whose attachment to region, language, or religion superseded national loyalties. American students are most likely to be familiar with the struggles within European nations over language or religion (e.g., the conflict between the various Celtic groups and the majority group in Great Britain; see Hecter 1975), but similar difficulties in trying to establish national identification were found in Asia as well.

In nineteenth century China, for example, individuals did not extend much loyalty beyond their family, lineage, or the peasant village. Because of differences in dialect, Chinese from one part of the country normally could not communicate with those from another region (see, e.g., Fei 1939; Freedman 1964; Johnson 1962; Nee and Wong 1985). In contrast, during this same period there was a considerable amount of travel and communication between Japanese villages. Even though individuals identified with their local prefecture (province) they did see themselves as part of a larger Japanese nation (Reischauer 1981, 32–37).

To get a true appreciation of the advantage the Japanese immigrants enjoyed because of their legacy of peoplehood, it is useful to compare their situation with that of the typical immigrants from Europe to American cities during the same time period. The historian Oscar Handlin (1951) points out that, contrary to conventional wisdom, most of the peasants who arrived from Europe in the nineteenth and early twentieth centuries did not see themselves as members of what today we would call their ethnic groups:

> Yet it was no easy matter then to define the nature of such groupings. Much later, in deceptive retrospect, a man might tell his children, Why we were Poles and stayed that way—or Italians, or Irish or German or Czechoslovaks. The memories were in error. These people had arrived in the New World with no such identification. The terms referred to national states not yet in existence or just come into being. The immigrants defined themselves rather by the place of their birth, the village, or else by the provincial region that shared dialect and custom; they were Masurians or Corkonians or Apulians or Bohemians or Bavarians. The parents back across the Atlantic, troubled by a son's too quick abandonment of the old ways, begged that he keep in himself the feeling of a Poznaniak (they did not say Pole). [1951, 186]

The absence of clear national identities meant that a major task for the "political entrepreneurs" in the European immigrant enclaves was to *create* a sense of "peoplehood." One of the major barriers facing these organizers was to convince people who were used to relating only to family, church, and village that they should become involved in larger scale associations. Eventually, in urban areas, this was resolved with the development of the "political machine." This essentially recreated aspects of the peasant village environment at the local level through the highly personalistic role of the precinct captain who dispensed "favors" and advice to the faithful voters. In turn, these local units were connected to one another by city- or county-wide party organizations. Nonetheless, as studies of the European immigrant experience amply illustrate, the task of developing social as well as political organization in the initially disorganized immigrant enclaves was extremely difficult and time consuming (see, e.g., Banfield and Wilson 1963, 117–118; O'Brien 1975, 35–40).

By contrast, the Japanese immigrants not only arrived in the

United States with a clear sense of national identity, but they also possessed a great deal of experience in participating in formal organizations. While it is true that these immigrants, like their European counterparts, had their closest attachments to their kin, village, and region (prefecture), they nonetheless possessed an overriding awareness that they were Japanese. This shared sense of history, culture, and fate provided them with a distinct advantage in relation to other groups when it came to developing strategies for organizing to deal with the unique problems they faced in the American experience.

Their capacity to organize collectively was especially evident, as we will see later, in the development of what has been called the vertically integrated "ethnic economy" in West Coast agriculture (Light 1972; Modell 1977; O'Brien and Fugita 1982). This very successful economic arrangement, in which the majority of the ethnic community was involved in some aspect of agricultural production and distribution, from growing to distribution to retail sales, was made possible in part by the fact that the individuals involved knew, understood, and above all *trusted* one another because they belonged to a single overarching ethnic community (see, e.g., Fugita and O'Brien 1991, chap. 3; Light 1972; O'Brien and Fugita 1982).

The sense of trust stemmed from participating in a type of social organization in Japan whose essentials were capable of being transferred to a variety of situations. The core principle of this social organization, and indeed the core principle of "Japaneseness," was a set of rules for facilitating relationships between people and ensuring the harmony of group relations.

It is true, of course, that the Japanese experienced periods of intense internal strife during their long history. What is striking about the Japanese experience, however, is that eventually conflicts between various warlords and factions were resolved through the creation of a complex set of rules for interaction and sharply defined role relationships that emphasized the priority of the group over the individual (Connor 1977; Weisz et al. 1984; Yamamoto and Wagatsuma 1980; Zander 1983).

The closest approximation to the nineteenth century Japanese social order in the Western experience is medieval feudalism, at least to the extent that both systems emphasized hierarchical relationships and the use of elaborate rituals to maintain them. However, while Western feudalism was essentially a very localistic system (see Fromm 1941, 40–44; Nisbet 1962, 25–32), Japanese feudalism encouraged the development of superior-subordinate relationships into larger and larger social groupings. This is seen especially in the development of the institution of the *iemoto* or "master-disciple" relationship. The principle behind the iemoto is described by Hsu:

> Each master has several disciples with whom he maintains mutual dependence. He commands great authority over his disciples. He owes to them the best he has to offer (livelihood, instruction, justice, social responsibility), and most of whatever he requires. The relationship and its characteristic ideas are not economic nor political, nor militaristic, nor religious. They can be applied to any field of endeavor, whether it be running a bean paste factory or an army or a university. [1971, 38]

The iemoto creates what Hsu (1971) terms "pseudo-kinship" relationships. This means that as people move away from their family of origin into schools, factories, or other organizations, they will relate to other persons in those organizations as if they were in some sense kin. Presumably individuals have choices with regard to which organizations they join, as for example when students select a particular school or workers a particular factory. The critical point, however, is that once a person becomes a member of such an organization s/he also enters a relationship that is closer to being a "relative" than a party to a limited contract. This provides a kind of "intimacy" in Japanese organizations which is not typically found in their Western counterparts. Hsu observes that

> although a majority of Japanese individuals have to move away from their first kinship base, their culture enables them to secure permanent circles of intimacy without moving too far way from it. And the all-inclusive and interlinking mutual dependence between members of any two levels in a large hierarchical organization has the effect of extending the feeling of intimacy beyond those situated near each other. [Hsu 1971, 38]

In short, feudalism in the Japanese case, in contrast to its effect in Europe, fostered a strong sense of national identity among ordinary Japanese citizens, and it had a profound effect on the whole pattern of adaptation and later assimilation of Japanese immigrants in the United States. Because the Japanese had the cultural templates for collective action it was quite natural for them to establish extensive networks of formal voluntary associations (Embree 1939, 112–157, 163–170; Norbeck 1972). In turn, their ability to better organize members of their group gave the Japanese immigrants a significant competitive advantage over other groups in certain types of business enterprises. This can be seen especially in the agricultural sector where the social organization of the ethnic community provided the infrastructure for critical economic linkages (Light 1972; Modell 1977; O'Brien and Fugita 1982).

Another important contribution of the legacy from Japan to the adaptation of the immigrants to life in America was the sense of "cultural relativism." Reischauer observes that, even in Japan today,

> the Japanese certainly have less of a sense of sin than Westerners or of a clear and inflexible line of demarcation between right and wrong. There are no obviously sinful areas of life. Most things seem permissible in themselves, so long as they do not do some damage in other ways. Moderation is the key concept, not prohibition. There is no list of "Thou Shalt Nots." [1981, 141–142]

Cultural relativism, however, must be understood in relation to the Japanese preoccupation with group survival. In fact, this relativism is so prevalent precisely because the survival of the group is the supreme ethical standard. Thus, in traditional Japanese ethics things are neither good nor bad in themselves, but are judged only insofar as they affect the harmony of interpersonal relations. In short, cultural relativism in the Japanese case does not mean that there is an absence of ethical principles, but rather that the standard for judging rightness or wrongness is group survival.

While one might take issue with Japanese style cultural relativism as a premise for an ethical system, it is clearly a very adaptive principle for group survival. In Japan this has led to a willingness to selectively incorporate the features of other peoples' cultures when it will help the group adapt to a changing world. This was seen, for example, in the incorporation of many elements of Chinese culture over the centuries and, during the nineteenth and twentieth centuries, in the adoption of significant elements of Western educational systems and technology (Reischauer 1981, 44–51; 228–230).

The fact that the incorporation of these "foreign" elements into Japanese culture did not weaken the integrity of the Japanese social system is not surprising if one understands the principle of cultural relativism in the Japanese historical experience. Foreign elements will weaken a traditional culture only if that culture postulates that the items which are replaced are essential to its integrity and survival. In the Japanese case, however, specific cultural items such as food, language, or even religion are not seen as essential to the survival of the group. Rather, it is the preservation of the group which is foremost in the Japanese psyche.

This explains, then, what appears to many Westerners as a curious paradox or even inconsistency in Japanese life. Although the Japanese take extraordinary pains to regulate the most minute details of interpersonal relations with complex rules, they have no difficulty at all in incorporating diverse elements of different religions into their devotional practices (Reischauer 1981, 224).

The principle of cultural relativism, or more accurately the ethical primacy of group survival over specific cultural content, such as religion, dress, or language, provided an additional advantage for the Japanese immigrants over their counterparts from other parts of the world. Although the Japanese initially entered North America as people who were perceived as more different from the native Anglo-Saxon inhabitants than the immigrants from Southern and Eastern Europe, their ability to move rapidly into the mainstream of American cultural and social life once discriminatory barriers were removed is really not terribly surprising given the core characteristics of Japanese culture which we have just described. Thus, for example, dressing like other Americans, adopting American recreational habits, and even practicing conventional American Protestant beliefs was not very much out of character for people from a culture which encouraged adaptability if it helped the survival of the group. In the larger sense, this adaptability is perhaps best reflected in the apparent contradiction between their assimilation into mainstream American life and the concomitant retention of a much more viable ethnic community life, in terms of actual involvement in ethnic voluntary associations, than is found in many other ethnic groups (see Fugita and O'Brien 1991).

REASONS FOR EMIGRATION

From early in the seventeenth century until well into the nineteenth, emigration from Japan was prohibited by law. This, along with a prohibition against immigration into the country, reflected the desire of the Tokugawa Shogunate (1615–1867) to isolate Japan from the rest of the world. The beginning of the end of this self-imposed separation came in 1854 when Admiral Perry's warships sailed into Edo (Tokyo) Bay. It was a show of military might that forced the Japanese government to open up its ports to Western nations and to enter into specific trade agreements. After being so directly confronted with Western military strength and observing the domination of China by Western powers because of the latter's technological superiority, the Japanese leaders wholeheartedly embraced Western ideas and technology (Moriyama 1984; 1985). Their decision, which spelled the end of the isolationist Tokugawa Shogunate and resulted in the emergence of the Meiji Restoration (1868–1912), illustrates a typical Japanese way of dealing with new exigencies. As in an earlier period when they adopted significant elements of Chinese culture, and during the post World War II period when they adopted Western ideas of government and fashion—some forcibly—the nineteenth century Japanese were able to incorporate ideas and practices from the outside without altering their basic forms of social organization (see Reischauer 1981, 228–230). As will be evident later, the same survival mechanism was employed by the Japanese immigrants in America.

In any event, in order to support the newly adopted Western-style industrialization, the Japanese government in 1873 substantially increased land taxes, shifting from the traditional method of taxing a percentage of crops produced to a new method of calculating taxes based on the value of the land itself. This placed a disproportionately heavy burden on farmers, with the result that between 1883 and 1890, 367,000 farmers were pushed off the land.

A substantial number of those who remained were forced into tenancy arrangements (Ike 1947).

In addition, government spending to suppress the Satsuma Rebellion in 1877 and to finance the Sino-Japanese War of 1894–95 created inflationary pressures which further reduced farmers' incomes. Moreover, the opening up of Japanese markets to foreign goods at a time when the Japanese themselves were underindustrialized and thus unable to compete effectively resulted in a substantial trade deficit which the government dealt with by circulating more money, thus stimulating inflation even more (Moriyama 1984).

The economic pressures just described forced many small farmers to seek alternative ways of bolstering sagging family incomes. Some left agriculture to work in the silk industry, which was one of the areas where Japan could compete in world markets. Others chose to labor in remote mines and factories (Sumiya 1963). Still others, following the traditional practice of *dekasegi rodo,* made the decision to leave home temporarily and work in distant places. In the earlier Tokugawa era, a number of farmers temporarily left the countryside to work on labor contracts in the towns and cities. This practice became quite common as the demand for labor increased during the period of rapid industrial expansion in the latter part of the nineteenth century. The historical precedent for temporarily migrating from home and then returning after earning money in a distant city established the concept of the "sojourner" in Japanese culture (Moriyama 1984; Bonacich and Modell 1980). Migration from the countryside to foreign lands, with the clear intent of staying temporarily and then returning home, was therefore a logical extension of the dekasegi rodo tradition.

Finally, two other roughly simultaneous events further increased the attraction of emigration. First, Japan's national conscription law, which took effect in 1873, encouraged young men to go abroad; if they were able to stay out of the country until the age of thirty-two they would then be ineligible for the draft. Moreover, if the oldest son in a family went overseas a younger son would be designated as the head of the household and thus escape military service as well (Ichihashi 1932; Moriyama 1984).

Second, with the advent of its open-door policy with respect to trade and cultural communication with foreigners, Japanese government officials began to receive requests for workers from other nations, including Australia, Canada, Hawaii, the West Indies, Spain, and the United States. With the single exception of permitting a small number of pearl divers and shellers to work for the British on an island north of Australia in 1883, the Japanese government had rejected these requests until 1885. At that point, the government changed its policy toward the emigration of contract workers, perhaps in part in response to the plight of the small farmers at that time, and became very actively involved in sponsoring contract laborers.

During the period from 1885 to 1894 the Japanese government had a virtual monopoly in the contract labor business, including a carefully supervised program of emigration to Hawaii. In 1894, with the passage of the Emigration Protection Ordinance, private interests were allowed to become brokers of contract laborers, but even during this period the government remained very much involved in the lives of emigrants both before and after they left Japan. In particular, Japanese leaders saw themselves as having responsibility to ensure that Japanese citizens were not mistreated overseas (Moriyama 1984).

In comparison to most other nations at the turn of the century, the Japanese government was much more actively involved in protecting the rights of its citizens. For instance, in 1903 a U.S. Government official noted that "the government of Japan closely supervises and regulates every detail of immigration" (U.S. Commissioner of Labor 1903, 36). This was partly designed to eliminate abuses which would eventually result in a reduced amount of emigration and, in turn, a decline in the amount of remittances which the emigrants returned to their families and the Japanese economy. It was in part also a result of the power Japan had recently gained vis-à-vis other nations following its defeat of China (1894–1895) and Russia (1904–1905). This power was reflected in the fact that President Theodore Roosevelt personally intervened in several local and state issues in California where nativist groups were attempting to restrict the personal liberties of Japanese immigrants. In one case an attempt was made to force Japanese children to attend segregated Chinese schools in San Francisco; in another, to restrict Japanese ownership of land through alien land laws. Eventually, powerful economic interests on the West Coast were able to succeed in passing alien land laws. And of course the civil liberties of the Issei and their American-born Nisei offspring were tragically violated during the incarceration. But the fact that American presidential influence was exerted at the turn of the century reflected a real concern at that time that relationships with the powerful Japanese nation not be adversely affected by immigration policy (Ichihashi 1932, 230, 261–262).

ONE

THE EARLY YEARS

 The vast majority of immigration from Japan to Hawaii and the West Coast of the United States took place during less than four decades, from 1885 to 1924. In 1924, the Immigration Exclusion Act virtually ended immigration until after World War II. During the early postwar years, a small number of Japanese women entered the country as brides of American servicemen who had served in the occupation force. From 1952 to 1965, a token quota was allowed in under the McCarran-Walter Immigration Bill.

Not until the major immigration reform of 1965, when Eastern Hemisphere countries were allocated quotas similar to those in the Western Hemisphere, could the Japanese immigrate to this country in significant numbers once again. However, even though legal impediments have been lifted, the flow of Japanese immigrants has been quite low, principally because of Japan's rapid economic growth during this period. Currently, fewer than five thousand Japanese a year immigrate to the U.S. There is an economically important population of Japanese nationals in the United States who are temporary residents working for Japanese multinational corporations. Owing to their strong company ties and the cultural gap between them and Japanese Americans, however, there is little meaningful interaction between the two groups. Nevertheless, their firms have used their financial resources to invigorate Japanese American cultural and economic institutions, particularly in Hawaii and California.

14

The narrow 1885–1924 window of immigration is significant both for scholars who study them and for Japanese Americans themselves. It has created very distinct cohorts of immigrant and American-born generations, each with its own unique set of historical experiences. This is perhaps best reflected in the certitude with which Japanese Americans, historians, and sociologists associate the distinctive experiences of the first, second, and third generations with the terms Issei, Nisei, and Sansei. One sociologist, Darrel Montero, points out that "the Japanese are the only ethnic group to emphasize geogenerational distinctions by a separate nomenclature and a belief in the unique character structure of each generational group" (1980, 8).

The vast majority of Japanese who immigrated to Hawaii and the West Coast of the United States came from four southwestern prefectures, Hiroshima, Yamaguchi, Fukuoka, and Kumamoto. Contrary to what we might expect, these were not the poorest areas of Japan during that period. It is true that the farms in Hiroshima were, on average, the smallest in the country, with 70 percent being less than 1.9 acres, but the size of the farms in the other three prefectures was close to the national average (Moriyama 1985).

These prefectures did, however, have an experienced agricultural labor force, part of which was prompted to emigrate through active recruiting by labor contractors. Once some workers ventured overseas, they encouraged others from the same area to follow. A study conducted in the Wakayama prefecture found that among 432 prospective emigrants, 25 percent said that their reason for wanting to go overseas was seeing their neighbors leave and then return with substantial amounts of money; 19 percent indicated that their reason for going was the "prevailing tendency in their village to emigrate"; and another 11 percent responded that they were "exhorted by emigrants residing abroad." These three reasons, which totaled 55 percent of the responses to the survey, outranked the 21 percent who simply said they were seeking wealth and the 19 percent who were "trying to better their lives." Although the rumors about large sums of money being made in Hawaii and the U.S. often were exaggerated, there is no doubt that higher wages could be earned overseas. The folk wisdom of the day suggested that a worker going to Hawaii could earn "400 yen in three years." This was a very large amount of money at that time and meant, in effect, that the emigrant could return a rich man (Moriyama 1985).

There were, however, a number of important differences between Hawaii and the mainland. The major portion of Japanese immigrants to Hawaii in the 1880s and 1890s were contract laborers who were sought by the sugar plantations to fill critical unskilled jobs. Between 1886 and 1899, 80,000 Japanese laborers entered Hawaii; by 1900, persons of Japanese ancestry comprised 39.7 percent of the total population of the Islands (Ichihashi 1932, 27). The descendants of these early settlers now constitute the largest ethnic community in Hawaii and dominate politics and public bureaucracies (Kitano 1976, 174–179). As we will see later, the size as well as the economic implications of removing the Japanese American population in Hawaii made it virtually impossible for the U.S. government to intern them as it did those on the West Coast during World War II.

The situation of the Japanese who immigrated to the mainland during the late nineteenth and early twentieth centuries was different in two significant ways. First, unlike the Hawaiian Japanese, they were a numerically small proportion of the population in the areas in which they settled. Even today in the Los Angeles area, which has the highest concentration of Japanese Americans on the mainland, persons in this ethnic group comprise less than 1 percent of the total population. This, as we will see in more detail in the next chapter, put the mainland Japanese in a much more vulnerable economic and political position vis-à-vis the white majority than was the case in Hawaii.

The second way in which the Japanese on the mainland differed from their Hawaiian counterparts was in their educational and occupational backgrounds. While most of the immigrants to Hawaii were contract laborers, a substantial portion of the Japanese immigrants to the mainland, many of whom stopped in Hawaii first, were students and merchants (Ichihashi 1932, 67).

DIFFERENCES BETWEEN CHINESE AND JAPANESE IMMIGRATION

It is important to note several differences between the pattern of Japanese immigration and that of the Chinese, which has affected the development of their respective ethnic communities. The first is the time of their arrival in the United States. The peak period of pre–World War II Chinese immigration took place from 1848 to 1882, while the major wave of Japanese immigration occurred from 1885 to 1920. By 1880, slightly over one-quarter of a million Chinese (228,945, to be exact) had been admitted to the U.S. as immigrants while only 335 Japanese had entered up to that time (see appendix 1 for the relative sizes of the two Asian immigrant groups in different time periods). The Chinese came first for the California Gold Rush and later to help build the transcontinental railroad. At that time Japanese citizens were prohibited by their government from leaving Japan and only very small numbers reached the U.S.

As indicated by the 1890 Census, the number of Chinese admitted to the U.S. dropped precipitously (61,711 from 1881 to 1890 as compared with 14,799 from 1891 to 1900) as anti-Chinese sentiment began to build on the West Coast and with it restrictive immigration legislation. The hostile reaction to the Chinese was principally a function of their being perceived as unfair, cheap labor and an easy target for labor union agitation (Saxton 1971). With the passage of the Chinese Exclusion Act in 1882 they became the first people to be legally prevented, as a group, from coming to the United States.

Although at a later point the Japanese were to receive the same treatment, for a time they were in demand as replacements for the Chinese. Their numbers rose significantly, from 149 in the period from 1871 to 1880 to 2,270 from 1881 to 1890 to 25,942 from 1891 to 1900 and to 129,797 from 1901 to 1910. During the following decade, from 1911 to 1920, the number of Japanese immigrants fell to 83,837 and then dropped further in the 1921 to 1930 period to 33,462. There was virtually no Japanese immigration in the period from 1931 to 1940 (1,948) (see appendix 1 for additional figures).

In part, the large increase in Japanese immigrants reported for the period from 1901 to 1910 was the result of the annexation of the Hawaiian Islands by the United States. All of the persons who had arrived earlier in what were then the Sandwich Islands were now recorded as immigrants. The choking off of virtually all immigration after 1920 was the result of the so-called Gentlemen's Agreement between Washington and Tokyo, the stopping of picture brides by the Japanese government, and the 1924 Exclusion Act which ended immigration until after World War II (Ichihashi 1932, 61–63).

Another interesting comparison between the Chinese and Japanese immigrants was their distribution in the American workforce. According to the 1900 Census, almost three times as many Japanese (62.2%) as Chinese (23.7%) were engaged in agriculture. By this time, many Chinese who had previously been farm laborers had moved into manufacturing and mechanical occupations and were represented in that work at a rate more than twice that of the Japanese (13.9% compared to 5.1%). Also, a greater proportion of the Chinese workforce was engaged in domestic and personal service work (51.2% compared to 22.0%). Overall, the Japanese immigrant population became disproportionately engaged in rural occupations and lifestyles whereas the Chinese became more involved in urban occupations and lifestyles (see appendixes 5 and 6). This difference has had important consequences for the long-term development of their respective communities. To this day, Chinese ethnic community life tends to have an urban cultural character whereas Japanese ethnic community life still draws heavily upon its rural roots, even though today most Japanese Americans live in metropolitan areas.

Finally, although the initial immigration of both the Chinese and the Japanese was to the West Coast, important differences in subsequent immigration and internal migration patterns have produced different densities of the respective ethnic groups in different areas of the country. The Japanese, by and large, have remained in the Western region of the country. Even as late as 1980, over 80 percent of Japanese Americans resided in that region. A majority of persons of Chinese ancestry also reside in the West, but that percentage (52.7%) is much smaller. Over one-fourth (26.8%) of the Chinese population lives in the East compared with a mere 6.5 percent for the Japanese (see appendix 2 for more details). These differences are due in part to the historical differences in occupational niches occupied by the two ethnic groups and in part by a post–World War II immigration of substantial numbers of Chinese who have settled outside of the West (see appendix 3 for more details on immigration).

18

THE JAPANESE IN CALIFORNIA AGRICULTURE

As noted earlier, the first substantial immigration of Japanese to California began during the period from 1900 to 1910, some ten to twenty years after the initial waves of immigration to Hawaii (Ichihashi 1932; U.S. Immigration Commission 1911). At that time there was an increased demand for farm labor, brought on by the exclusion of the Chinese, the movement of white workers into nonagricultural work, and the increased scale and productivity of intensive agriculture resulting from government-subsidized irrigation projects and new railroad car refrigeration techniques (Agricultural Labor in California 1940). These developments coincided with the economic problems facing small farmers in Japan. Thus both a push and a pull motivated the immigrants.

One of the most striking aspects of the Japanese immigrants' adaptation to California agriculture was their ability to collectively organize to meet their economic needs. As in the rural villages in Japan, the problems facing the immigrants were interpreted more in "collective" than "individualistic" terms (Embree 1939, 112–157; Ichihashi 1932, 172). Moreover, the Japanese were quite well educated for immigrants and thus often recognized when they were being exploited. When they felt they were being mistreated, they frequently struck or left for other work. This led farmers who employed Japanese labor crews to view them as more aggressive than the Chinese they had replaced (Ichihashi 1932, 68–78; Beechert 1977; Light 1972, 74–75; U.S. Department of Labor 1945, 52).

A factor which permitted Japanese farm laborers to be more aggressive toward the farmers they worked for was the interpersonal nature of their labor contractor system. As was the case in other ethnic groups, Japanese labor contractors sometimes took advantage of their fellow countrymen—e.g., by assessing daily commissions, charging "translation-office fees," selling expensive provisions, charging for remitting money to Japan, and withholding a medical fee (Ichioka 1988; Yoneda 1967). But because they were embedded in other social relationships with the same individuals in the Japanese community, the more serious forms of exploitation would result in ostracism from the community. This tended to reduce exploitation substantially.

The labor contractor–worker relationship was also supported by the traditional Japanese principle of iemoto (Hsu 1975), which emphasized the obligations of superiors toward subordinates as much as those of lower echelon persons to their superiors. This principle of organization, which rested on Confucian ethics and had been a part of Japanese everyday life for several centuries, in effect created a quasi-kin relationship between Japanese of different ranks in hierarchical organizations (see Ichihashi 1932, 175; Light 1972, 74; Modell 1977, 63–69).

Not surprisingly, then, the Japanese played a significant role in efforts to organize farm laborers at the turn of the century (U.S. Department of Labor 1945, 51–54). In 1908, for example, Japanese laborers formed the Higher Wages Association to gain better wages and parity with European workers on Hawaiian plantations (Beechert 1977). In the same year, a socialist Japanese labor union, the Fresno Rodo Domei Kai (Fresno Labor League), with an estimated 2,000 members, was successful in constricting the flow of Japanese laborers to the few labor contractors who cut the rate agreed upon by the Japanese labor contractors organization (the Central California Contractors Association) (Ichioka 1971).

Moreover, alliances were formed between the Japanese and workers of other nationalities (Beechert 1977). In five of the forty-nine labor disputes during the first decade of the twentieth century in Hawaii there was cooperation between Japanese and other nationalities. The first farm workers' union in California was the result of a strike by 1,000 Japanese and Mexican sugar beet workers in Oxnard in 1903. The Japanese, the first to organize and strike, were later joined by the Mexican workers. Together they formed the Sugar Beet and Farm Laborers' Union of Oxnard, with a Japanese president and vice president and a Mexican secretary (Foner 1964; U.S. Department of Labor 1945, 52–53; Yoneda 1967).

Later there was some involvement of Japanese workers in farm union activity, such as the Japanese Farm Workers Union, formed in 1935, which provided leadership for the Venice celery strike of 1936 (Tsuchida 1978). Nevertheless, in California the overall trend after the first decade of the twentieth century was a lessening of Japanese involvement in unionization efforts.

A major factor in diminishing Japanese enthusiasm for union activity was the blatant racism of the American Federation of Labor

(Modell 1969). When the Sugar Beet and Farm Laborers' Union of Oxnard applied for membership in the AFL, for example, Samuel Gompers replied, "Your union must guarantee that it will under no circumstances accept membership of any Chinese or Japanese" (Foner 1964, 276–277). Although at one point the AFL's California Central Labor Council attempted to reduce hostility toward Asians in order to expedite the organization of farm workers, the racist position prevailed during most of the time Japanese immigrants worked in the fields. Indeed, in one incident in Fresno in 1911, AFL organizers attempted to unionize white workers for the specific purpose of replacing Japanese workers (U.S. Department of Labor 1945, 58). The radical Industrial Workers of the World (IWW) was much more favorably disposed toward Asian laborers, but it was destroyed as a union during the "Red Scare" in 1917 (U.S. Department of Labor 1945, 59–69; Yoneda 1967).

While the opportunity for Japanese farm laborers to participate in mainstream union activities was severely limited by racism on the West Coast, it is also true that the Japanese community as a whole tended to discourage this route to upward mobility and instead to foster entrepreneurial values. For instance, the socialist Fresno Rodo Domei Kai faced a hostile Japanese language press and claims by ethnic community spokesmen that it was an anarchist organization (Ichioka 1971). This entrepreneurial outlook was, of course, consistent with the sojourner mentality of the Issei which focused on quickly making a small fortune and then returning to Japan.

There were, however, differences between the Hawaiian and West Coast situations with respect to the opportunities they offered for the realization of small business aspirations and, in turn, the attractiveness of union activity. In Hawaii an entrenched plantation system did not offer the Japanese immigrants the options of sharecropping, leasing, and independent farming which were available on the West Coast. Thus, prior to World War II the Japanese in Hawaii were much more involved in unions and radical politics than were their counterparts on the mainland.

In any event, the typical situation in California was one in which the Issei eventually came to work his own land, either through direct ownership, leasing, or sharecropping. What is perhaps most striking in historical accounts of these farmers is the extent to which they were willing to work on land which most Caucasians would have seen as not suitable for raising crops. One observer during this time describes the Issei approach to the land:

> The Japanese, like the Chinese earlier and now, have been willing to pay higher rents than others for land—such high rents in fact that the owner has frequently found it more profitable to lease his land than to farm it on his own account. That the Japanese and Chinese can afford to pay a relatively high rent is explained in part by the fact that their efficiency and the kinds of crops grown by them will bear it, in part by the fact that they have a different standard of application, and in part by the fact that the income in prospect for farming need not be so large as that expected by most farmers. The Asiatic farmer expects to work hard and for long hours, the Japanese is usually assisted in garden or field by his wife if he has one, the opportunities for employment other than as an unskilled laborer have been limited, and as a result of careful and efficient growing of intensive crops his return per acre is ordinarily a large one. [Millis 1915]

From the very outset, the capacity of the Japanese to be productive in farming proved to be a mixed blessing. On the one hand, it clearly contributed to their economic mobility and their eventual movement into middle class occupations (e.g., Fujimoto 1975), but, at the same time, it caused a good deal of resentment on the part of many white farmers who saw them as unfair competitors. This supported prejudicial attitudes which eventually resulted in a series of alien land laws intended to drive the Issei out of farming, push them back into a farm laboring status, and discourage future immigration. California Attorney General U. S. Webb, one of the coauthors of the first Alien Land Act passed in the state, stated that the objective was "to limit their presence by curtailing their privileges which they may enjoy here; for they will not come in large numbers and long abide with us if they may not acquire land" (Chuman 1976, 48).

The first attempts by California legislators to introduce legislation to restrict Japanese in agriculture were made in 1907. The most important impetus for this was provided by small farmers who wanted to squash what they perceived to be unfair competition. The following testimony, given by Attorney General Webb in argument against naturalization for the Japanese, reflects, in polite language, many of their feelings:

> The American family reared along the lines of American traditions with the father managing the farm, the mother presiding in the home, and the children during their younger years attending school, cannot compete with the Oriental farm life wherein children and mother join with the father in the actual farm labor, and in addition do not enjoy conditions of life which are demanded by the American standard of living. [Brief of the Attorney General of California 1922]

Many large growers opposed the attempts to limit the ability of the Japanese to lease land since they found it more profitable to lease their land to them than to grow crops themselves. If such a law was passed, however, it would make available to them a larger farmworker labor pool. Also, some local politicians in California seized upon the land law issue for political reasons.

Initially, legislation was introduced which would have prevented all aliens from owning land. Protests from representatives of several European countries and foreign investors, however, made it unlikely that a bill of this nature could pass. Thus, the legislators adopted the strategy of not directly naming the Japanese, but singling them out by making the law applicable only to "aliens ineligible for citizenship." In order to placate the large landowners, the California Senate inserted a clause permitting the Japanese to lease land for three years. The bill was overwhelmingly passed in 1913.

The California law posed a serious problem for President Wilson's administration in Washington. Japan was militarily a powerful country and had important trade relationships with the U.S. Thus, Washington did not want to cause unnecessary offense. Japanese Ambassador Chinda lodged three protests against the law.

Many Easterners could not understand why Californians wanted to discriminate against such a small minority. When word of the possible passage of the law reached Japan, there were mass protests in Tokyo and even calls for war. This disturbed Wilson enough to dispatch his secretary of state, William Jennings Bryan, to Sacramento. Bryan's mission was to try to persuade Californians of the importance of taking into account national interests before deciding to pass legislation with such international implications.

Because the Democratic administration had been elected with a states' rights plank in 1912, however, Wilson was constrained from using the more heavy-handed approach employed by his predecessor Theodore Roosevelt in dealing with the San Francisco Oriental school issue which had resulted in the so-called Gentlemen's Agreement of 1906–7. As it turned out, Bryan's mission was unsuccessful and perhaps even counterproductive. California's Progressive Republican legislators were not about to be pressured by the federal government again (Bailey 1932).

Unfortunately for its advocates, the Japanese were able to get around the 1913 law and continue farming because of the wide legal loopholes. Some Issei put the land in the name of their American-born children and made themselves their guardians. Or they placed land in the name of legal-age children, usually Hawaiian-born Nisei, some of whom were just beginning to reach their majority, or less often used the name of sympathetic white friends. Some Issei created dummy corporations which had a majority of American citizen shareholders. One common arrangement was to have their Nisei children, a white lawyer, and themselves as stockholders. If there were two children, the lawyer, and the Issei farmer and his wife, citizens would outnumber the "aliens ineligible for citizenship" (Higgs 1978).

The initiative process was used in 1920 to try to close the loopholes of the 1913 law. This extremely restrictive bill, which was passed by the voters in every county in California, prohibited the Issei from owning or leasing land, being corporation shareholders, or acting as guardians for minors owning or leasing land. Because it directly threatened the very livelihood of the majority of the members of the immigrant community, the Japanese filed a suit to challenge many of its provisions. Ultimately, the Supreme Court upheld the law in four test cases in 1923 (Carrot 1983; Ichioka 1984; 1988, 226–234).

As documented by Ichioka using Japanese language sources, the loss of these court decisions not only made it virtually impossible for the Japanese to legally farm in any manner, but deeply demoralized the community. The Japanese Counsel of San Francisco commented that

The land law decisions have dealt a severe blow to Japanese immigrants, spiritually as well as materially. . . . They had previously won a favorable decision . . . on cropping contracts. As lease agreements expired, the majority switched to these contracts. Nearly everyone anticipated victory in this case. Just at the point when they firmly believed that they could solve all land law difficulties through cropping contracts, the case ended in failure. The sense of despair it aroused is hard to imagine. [Ichioka 1984, 168]

Even though the 1920 law severely restricted farming among the Japanese, there remained one legal and several illegal techniques which could be used to get around its stranglehold. The legal avenue was adjudicated by the California Supreme Court in the *Estate of Tesubumi Yano* case in 1922. In this decision, the court held that the 1920 law could not prevent Issei from giving their land to their minor children for whom they acted as legal guardians and farm managers (Carrott 1983; Higgs 1978).

One of the most common illegal techniques involved collusion between the Japanese farmer and a Caucasian middleman. Here a farmer would have a citizen lease land for him. The Issei would do all of the actual farming. The middleman would hire the Issei farmer as a manager or foreman. This technique, however, placed the farmer in a precarious position. If the middleman raised his fees or died, the farmer would be seriously compromised (Ichioka 1984).

Another way the Issei could get around the law was to make an oral agreement directly with the landowner. Publicly, the landowner would hire the farmer as his foreman. Privately, the farmer was treated as a lessee or share tenant. Consistent with their earlier opposition to the alien land laws, some landowners found it profitable to lease land to the Japanese and thus were amenable to such an arrangement. Again, however, it was risky for the Japanese farmer, particularly if the local district attorney was enforcing the law (Ichioka 1984).

Another possibility was to create a land corporation similar to the one previously described, except that it would be formed specifically to serve as the lessee for a group of farmers. A farmer would have the corporation lease a viable plot of land and he in turn would lease it from the corporation. The corporation, then, would publicly hire the farmer as a foreman. The secretary of the local Japanese association would act as the manager of the company, dealing with the landowners and handling all of the necessary business transactions for a small percentage. This strategy for dealing with the 1920 land law was the most secure from the farmer's perspective, and it was legal as long as the accounting was maintained and taxes paid (Ichioka 1988, 239–240).

A number of scholars have attempted to assess the impact of the extremely discriminatory and restrictive 1920 law on the subsequent involvement of the Japanese in California agriculture. They have, however, come to widely varying conclusions on the law's long range impact (e.g., Daniels 1974, 88; Higgs 1978; Ichihashi 1932, 277–282; Ichioka 1984; Ichioka, 1988, 234–235; Iwata 1962; McWilliams 1944, 65). A major reason for the difficulty in reaching a definitive conclusion is that the data from that time period are of unknown reliability. In addition, since agricultural activities go through normal cycles and the number of Issei decreased by about one-third from 1920 to 1930, it is difficult to make accurate categorizations about the effect of the law on the number of Japanese who remained in farming.

Appendixes 11 and 12 show two tables compiled by Higgs (1978) which index Japanese involvement in California agriculture up to World War II. These data suggest that the 1920 law initially did constrain Japanese involvement in agriculture during the 1920s but that by the 1930s, when their American-born children were coming of age, the Japanese were in the main able to skirt the intent of the law. Nonetheless, scholars have pointed out that the Act continued to loom large as a threat to Japanese farmers:

> An alien, denied the right of citizenship, denied the right to own or lease land, and finding himself under continuous harassment, would think twice before investing hard-earned money in land which might be taken away from him at any time. [Kitano 1976, 19–20]

> The anti-alien land laws made land ownership speculative and unpredictable, subject to the pressure of the anti-Japanese leaders and the inclination of the district attorneys, rather than rational capital. [Miyakawa 1974, 108]

Several states followed California's lead in passing alien land laws, including some that had very small Japanese populations: Arizona in 1917; Louisiana, Nebraska, Texas, and Washington in 1921; New Mexico in 1922; Idaho, Montana, and Oregon in 1923; and Kansas in 1925 (Carrott 1983; Ichihashi 1932: 280).

Two features of the Issei's response to the alien land laws are central to understanding the broader Japanese American experience. First, their responses drew upon the organized resources of their ethnic community. Second, even though they faced de jure discrimination which attempted to deny them their livelihood, prevented them from ever becoming fully enfranchised Americans, and totally excluded the further immigration of their fellow countrymen to the United States, they were still able to build orderly and meaningful lives. It is clear that if they did not have the support of such a cohesive ethnic community for meeting both material and emotional/psychological needs, their lives would have been much more chaotic.

As noted earlier, models for collective organization had been present in Japanese culture for some time and they were used to develop rotating credit associations (*tanomoshi*), partnerships, and cooperatives in the United States. These mechanisms played an important role in the development of Japanese small businesses because they permitted the immigrants to bypass white credit and lending institutions, which often discriminated against them. A number of these collective organizations have persisted up to the present day, especially among Japanese growers in the fruit, vegetable, and flower industries (Embree 1939; Light 1972; Miyamoto 1939; Yoder 1936).

The role of Japanese culture in creating and maintaining these collective organizations is perhaps best illustrated in the institution of the tanomoshi or rotating credit association. The tanomoshi, like the *hui* in Chinese immigrant communities, was an association of persons who made regular contributions to a common economic "pot" whose goal was to provide the capital necessary to finance the startup or expansion of small businesses or other major purchases. Procedures varied from one tanomoshi to the other with respect to how individuals were chosen to get the money in the "pot." In some instances, lots were drawn; in others, a type of "bidding" procedure was used (Light 1972).

The underlying premise of the rotating credit association was that eventually every individual who contributed to the common pot would have a chance to use the money for a given time period. Obviously, some individuals experienced the benefits of the tanomoshi before others. Moreover, there was no legal recourse to get money back should those who benefited early elect not to return money into the common treasury. This problem was made all the more difficult for the Japanese by the fact that in their status as a persecuted minority they had very little real access to the legal system. Therefore, ultimately, the success of the tanomoshi depended upon the trust which individuals had in one another (Light 1972; Miyamoto 1939).

The basic source of the trust so critical for the functioning of the tanomoshi was family honor. This is an example of the quasi-kin relationships among the Japanese, rooted in the iemoto (Hsu 1975), which made it possible for family-type relationships to go beyond blood and marital connections. Light suggests that these kinds of relationships, which he calls "ascriptive ties," gave the tanomoshi a "moral significance" which ensured that individuals would meet their obligations to fellow members (1972, 60). This was reinforced by the fact that the members of the rotating credit association met regularly and used these occasions as opportunities to build social bonds with one another (Light 1972). It should be noted that if an individual was not known to the other members of the group, s/he had to be appropriately introduced by someone known to the group who was willing to vouch for the stranger.

The importance of Japanese culture in providing a basis of trust between individuals was found at many other levels in the development of the so-called ethnic economy in the nineteenth and early twentieth centuries. The strong sense of obligation, commitment, and family honor in their culture provided the motivation for family members to tolerate the long hours necessary in labor-intensive small business enterprises. In order to become successful in restaurants or truck farms, for example, everyone in the family had to be willing to work at what would be considered by most Americans, even in those days, very poor wage per hour rates. It is certainly true, of course, that part of the motivation here was the result of discrimination in precluding work options in other sectors of the economy. But it is also true, as in the case of other ethnic groups which have been successful in small business ventures, that family members had a clear sense that their efforts eventually would be rewarded either by gaining a share of the business, as in the case of children who would take over after the retirement or death of their parents, or by assistance in starting their own business venture at some future date. The critical point in all of these instances is that the payoff was not immediate. Again, the individual had to have a significant amount of trust in the workings of the overall social organization of the economic enterprise in order to believe that his/her efforts made any sense at all. As Light (1972) points out, it is the very fact that this kind of "social trust" is so difficult to achieve that explains why most ethnic groups have not been very successful in small businesses.

Moreover, this social trust among the Japanese was critical in ensuring smooth relationships between different ethnic enterprises which depended on one another in the various phases of the production and distribution process in agriculture. Among the Japanese growers, packers, shippers, and retailers in the Southern California truck farming market this social interconnectedness resulted in what Modell (1977) terms a "vertically integrated ethnic economy" (see also Bloom and Reimer 1949, 92–96). For example, Japanese farmers' cooperatives bought supplies at favorable prices, attempted to control labor rates in the local area, and regulated within group competition (e.g., Ichioka 1971).

In addition, traditional Japanese culture played an important role in ensuring the high quality of products which were sold to nonethnic buyers. Most of the purchases of the products grown on Japanese truck farms were made by non-Japanese. Thus, the cultural admonition to protect the honor of one's family and that of the Japanese people became an important lever which Japanese businessmen used to minimize unscrupulous practices by fellow ethnics and to prevent giving Japanese businessmen a bad name (e.g., Miyamoto 1939; Tsuchida 1978). In this way, the social pressures maintained by a well organized ethnic community served to provide a "public good" (see Olson 1971) for the entire ethnic community, in the form of the "good reputation" of Japanese as high quality producers of agricultural products.

Again, drawing upon the cultural principles of social organization brought with them from Japan, the Issei immigrants formed 100 "Japanese Associations." These organizations, however, were not merely transfers from Japan, but also products of the immigrants' and the Japanese government's efforts to adapt to conditions in America, especially anti-Japanese agitation (Fujita 1929; Ichioka 1977a). Among other things, these associations provided experts who visited the farmers in their jurisdiction, gave lectures and advice, and represented the growers in labor disputes. Books and pamphlets with titles such as *Report of Investigation on Arable Land* (1918) and *Report of the Investigation on Agricultural Land Outside the State* (1926) (Fujita 1929) were published, the latter in response to the restrictions placed on Japanese growers in California by the alien land laws.

Legal discrimination, boycotts, and other threats against Japanese entrepreneurs were sometimes met with concerted action by the larger Japanese American community (Kitano 1976, 21–22; Modell, 1977, 100–102). A classic illustration of this is found in the El Monte berry strike of 1933. Eighty percent of the 600 to 700 acres of berries in the El Monte area near Los Angeles were controlled by Japanese growers who belonged to the Central Japanese Association of Southern California. The Japanese farmers were struck by the Communist-organized Cannery and Agricultural Workers Union (CAWU), composed mainly of Mexican workers. The very few Japanese workers who joined the strike were ignored by the Japanese community. Japanese American youths were successful in getting excused from school in order to help their parents with the harvest, and their appeal was supported by the El Monte Chapter of the Japanese American Citizens League (JACL). In addition, large numbers of friends and relatives came to help out in the fields (Hoffman 1973; Lopez 1970; Modell 1977, 122; Spaulding 1934; Wollenberg 1972).

The El Monte berry strike also illustrates the unique relationships among Japanese farmers, the Japanese community, white landowners, and public officials. Because of the alien land laws, the Japanese immigrants faced severe restrictions in their ability to own land outright. Moreover, most of the lessees and lessors were in collusion to violate the law (as interpreted by the courts in 1923). This arrangement put the Issei farmers in a precarious legal, economic, and political situation. The district attorney could enforce the law at any time and there was enough enforcement in some areas, depending upon local political pressures and anti-Japanese sentiment, to maintain uncertainty among Japanese farmers (Ito 1973, 449–453). Moreover, if a conspiracy between the Japanese lessee and the white lessor could be proven, the lessor could lose his land.

White lessors, then, were threatened by the El Monte labor disturbance because it could focus attention on their profitable illegal arrangements. White agricultural interests also were concerned that if the Mexican laborers were successful against the Japanese they would walk out of their fields next (Wollenberg 1972). Not surprisingly, then, the white landowners, the El Monte and Los Angeles Chambers of Commerce, the Los Angeles Police Department, and the Los Angeles County Sheriff's Department supported the Japanese farmers in the strike (Modell 1977, 122–123).

Another example of ethnic community support for Japanese farmers is found in the Venice celery strike of 1936. Here approximately 800 Mexican, 200 Japanese, and a small number of Filipino celery pickers struck the growers in the Venice area. The Southern California Farm Federation, a Japanese growers' organization of 800 farmers, flatly rejected their wage and union recognition demands. The strike quickly spread to other locales in Los Angeles, affecting other crops grown by Japanese farmers. The Farm Federation received the support of the Los Angeles County Sheriff's Department, the Los Angeles and Culver City Police Departments, the U.S. Immigration Service, and the Japanese Consulate.

Because of the fear that the Japanese community would suffer severe economic losses, the major community organizations, such as the Central Japanese Association of Southern California, the Japanese Association of Los Angeles, the Little Tokyo Businessman's Association, a local vernacular newspaper, and the Orange County and Los Angeles chapters of the JACL endorsed the position of the growers. The Japanese Association of Los Angeles raised over $2,400 from other associations, banks, and firms for the purpose of crushing the sometimes violent strike. The only organizations to support the strikers were the Gardeners Association and the Rodo Kyoyukai (Laborers Cooperative and Friendly Society) (Tsuchida 1978).

Finally, the larger Japanese community supported the Issei farmers, packer/shippers, and fruit stand operators through a variety of mechanisms which reinforced the notion that ethnicity was linked to specific occupations. In 1935, for example, the JACL, with the support of other community organizations, sponsored an oratorical contest for the second generation Nisei with the theme "Japanese in Agriculture." Eleven Southern California JACL districts from San Luis Obispo to San Diego held preliminary contests in preparation for the finals, which were attended by over 800 people in a hot and crowded Little Tokyo church in Los Angeles. The principal reason for the event, according to historians, was that many of the Issei who were dependent upon the Japanese growers for their livelihood (they had developed a vertically integrated, highly interdependent grower linked to distributor linked to retailer ethnic economy) were very concerned about the exodus of Nisei from the farms to the city (Modell 1977, 94–126).

THE ROLE OF THE FAMILY IN ECONOMIC ADAPTATION

In the first two decades of Japanese immigration to the U.S., the sex ratio heavily favored men, some 2,369 to 100 in 1900 and 694 to 100 in 1910 (Lyman 1977). This was the "frontier period" of the Japanese community (Miyamoto 1939). Bachelor men worked mainly as farm and other types of laborers under a Japanese labor contractor. By 1907, the cries of "yellow peril" resulted in the so-called Gentlemen's Agreement which drastically reduced the flow of male immigrants. It did not, however, halt the influx of females. By 1920 the sex ratio was much more balanced, 189 males to 100 females (Thomas 1952). As Miyamoto (1939) has pointed out, this rapid increase in the number of wives and families signaled the beginning of the "settling period" of family and community building. This was the period when the Japanese community became highly organized.

World War I was characterized by rapid economic expansion in the nation at large. Many in the Japanese community took advantage of these economic opportunities to make the transition from wage labor to family businesses. This was facilitated by the fact that the Issei were familiar with the household as the unit of production and consumption in the farming villages from which most of them emigrated. In that setting, family and business were one domain (e.g., Yanagisako 1975).

The household or *ie* was critical in the economic accommodation of the Japanese since it made available to them an institution which legitimized the use of unpaid family labor, giving the Japanese a competitive advantage over the Chinese, who were much less likely to have family households in the United States during this period (Nee and Wong 1985). Moreover, family building among the Issei provided an incentive to successfully accommodate to American society on many dimensions. After all, the well-being of their American-born children was at stake. As the Nisei became more acculturated in the public schools, they in turn influenced their parents who were more isolated from the mainstream. Nee and Wong (1985) also suggest that the presence of families prevented the demoralization of the Issei males. They argue that the Chinese immigrants, largely males living alone, were more vulnerable to demoralization.

Another consequence of the family-based small business accommodation of the Issei is that it supported the retention of Japanese forms of social organization and provided a sense of continuity and stability from the old country to the new. For instance, the rule of primogeniture specified that the oldest son inherited the family farm and was responsible for the welfare of his aging parents. In Japan, this was tied to the economic necessity of keeping the small tracts of farmland intact to retain their economic viability. As long as the Issei worked in a family business which could be passed on to the eldest son, primogeniture and the eldest son's responsibilities for his aging parents could continue as it did in Japan (Yanagisako 1975; 1985).

COMMUNITY LIFE

Like all immigrant groups in the United States, the first generation Issei attempted to recreate many of the institutions and culture they had left behind. In some ways, the Japanese had an advantage over other more diverse immigrant groups in that they had a long tradition of being a culturally homogeneous people. We do not find among the Japanese, for example, the problem faced by many European immigrant groups of overcoming strong loyalties to region and dialect which made it difficult to form a single ethnic identification (e.g., Handlin 1951).

In addition, the Japanese also had a clear advantage over many other immigrant groups with respect to their experience in organizing and participating in organizations to deal with collective needs. In contrast to the difficulty leaders faced in convincing European peasants to participate in what were for them quite unfamiliar types of organizations (for most persons in these groups the only significant associations to which one belonged were family, kin, and perhaps the local church), Issei leaders were able to draw upon models which could readily be adapted to the problems of creating community in the New World. Moreover, unlike the experience of most European immigrant groups whose governments, by and large, had little to do with them once they left their homeland, the Japanese government continued to take an active interest in the fate of its citizens overseas, devoting considerable energy to the development and maintenance of quasi-governmental ties in the form of the Japanese Associations which were found in virtually all immigrant communities. It should be noted, however, that the Japanese government sometimes abandoned the interests of the immigrants when it was politically expedient to do so (Ichioka 1977a; 1977b).

The Issei also developed Buddhist churches, kenjinkai (prefectural associations), business groups (e.g., gardeners' and retailers' associations) and language schools to teach their children (the Nisei) the language and customs of Japan. The language schools are a classic example of the way the Japanese in America have dealt with the problem of preserving their community and its traditions. These schools were not parochial schools in the same sense as Catholic or Lutheran institutions, in that Japanese children did attend the public schools. However, they presented, in a very structured manner (usually by a stern teacher from Japan), many of the elements of Japanese culture, particularly those relating to social relationships and moral principles (Lebra 1972).

One additional "advantage" the Issei had over most European immigrant groups in recreating traditional community life was that they were more insulated from mainstream society by virtue of the more intense discrimination against them in employment and housing. Immigrants from Eastern and Southern Europe and the Irish were seen by white Anglo-Saxon Protestant "Native

Americans" as being of a lower order on the evolutionary scale; excessive numbers of them were thought to be threatening to the very survival of the Republic. Thus, the dominant thrust of mainstream institutions was to try to force the immigrants to abandon their old culture and to adopt what was viewed by the majority group as a superior culture (see Hofstadter 1955a, 1955b). In the case of the Japanese, however, the response of the majority group was to maintain some elements of de facto, and in some instances a clear de jure, segregation of the ethnic community from white society. The Japanese did not experience the kind of complete isolation enforced upon blacks, as illustrated by the fact that most Nisei children attended public schools with whites, but they did nonetheless live apart from white society in many significant ways.

Yet, at the same time, most Nisei, like the children of other immigrant groups, had an intense desire to be accepted as Americans. The result of this was that while the Issei generally clung to the old ways as much as they could, the Nisei lived in two worlds. They spent much of their time in the white world of school, but virtually all of their primary relationships were with fellow Japanese (Daniels 1985). Thus, they were not totally isolated from the main currents of American life, but their most intimate relationships and institutional affiliations were found within the ethnic community.

As might be expected, there were distinctive differences between Hawaii and the mainland with respect to the relationships between Japanese and white Americans. Both formal (e.g., alien land laws) and informal means of social exclusion could be effectively practiced against the relatively small minority in California and other West Coast states, but it simply was not possible in Hawaii where by the turn of the century the Japanese constituted the largest ethnic community and where all the Asian groups combined far outnumbered the whites. Therefore, even though a Caucasian minority retained a privileged landlord status vis-à-vis the Japanese and other Asian laborers, eventually the Japanese began to fill skilled trade positions and later semiprofessional and professional jobs, especially in public bureaucracies, such as elementary and secondary school systems.

This more benign environment differed sharply from the West

Coast situation where blatant discrimination against Japanese Americans in many sectors of the economy continued until after World War II. These differences in the experiences of Hawaiian and West Coast Japanese Americans vis-à-vis whites may account in part for what has become a noticeable difference in the demeanor of individuals in the two ethnic communities.

While the more "laid-back" interpersonal style of the Hawaiian "Buddhahead" is no doubt partly due to the general atmosphere of the Islands it is also a product of the fact that Hawaiian Japanese, unlike the mainland "Kotonk," have not been on the defensive for nearly as long. It is obviously easier for a Japanese person in such a situation to behave in a less controlled manner than it is for his/her mainland counterpart who has known (or whose parents have known) outright discrimination from a powerful majority (Kitano 1976, 164–169).

Nonetheless, even with the situational differences between Hawaii and the mainland, the kinds of Japanese values which the Issei passed on to their children were similar. The "relativistic" ethic, which historically has helped the Japanese adapt to changing conditions in Japan, also made it possible for the immigrants to adapt to a unique set of exigencies in the New World and yet maintain the integrity of the group. This part of Japanese culture permitted the emerging Japanese American communities to join American cultural content with Japanese organizational forms (see O'Brien and Fugita 1983a).

The Issei changed the day of the services in their Buddhist temples to Sunday in order to adapt to American church customs, and created Japanese associations and business groups which had agendas geared specifically to the American situation. At the same time, however, these associations were built on Japanese principles of social organization. The Nisei had few *intimate* contacts with persons other than fellow Japanese and yet they organized a whole range of activities with American content, such as basketball and bowling leagues as well as ballroom dancing clubs, within organizational frameworks that were traditionally Japanese. Here the young Nisei could feel comfortable doing American things and yet be socialized into Japanese ways of relating. Thus, the significant Japanese ways which have been passed from generation to generation are not language or even religion (the Japanese Christian churches often supplanted the Japanese Buddhist Churches), but the core values which maintain social relationships and a style of interaction that is distinctively Japanese.

TWO

PORTENTS OF THE INCARCERATION

 By the late 1930s, the Issei had established a viable niche for themselves in small business enterprises, especially in labor-intensive agriculture. This was in part an accommodation to the limitations imposed on them by the racism of the period which restricted their opportunities in other sectors of the economy, but it was also a product of a cultural world view which saw work as best dealt with collectively (Embree 1939). It was, in fact, this high level of ethnic interdependency which produced what some scholars have termed an "ethnic economy" (e.g., Light 1972). It should also be noted that the Japanese farmers were fortunate to be working in a part of the American economy which was less adversely affected than others by the Depression (Daniels 1985).

Even though they realized that it would be very difficult to get good jobs in the larger society, the Japanese felt that education was a way out of the arduous and low paying jobs in the ethnic economy. Many Issei reasoned that even if the Nisei could not get jobs in the larger society, they could at least become professionals who served the ethnic community. This outlook was supported by the experience of growing up in a small business household, such as a truck farm, which fostered values and a lifestyle conducive to high educational aspirations and the desire to become a professional or a manager (see, e.g., Bland, Elliot, and Bechhofer 1978; Fujimoto 1975).

Unfortunately, the Nisei often were not able to make full use of their educational achievements. For example, although they were generally high achievers in school and well thought of by their teachers, they were by and large excluded from public school teaching on the mainland even when they had acquired the necessary college training. Roger Daniels notes:

> Fully credentialed Nisei education majors, for example, were virtually unemployable as teachers in the very schools in which they had excelled. Whatever their skills, most Nisei were forced into the ethnic economic community; their parents expected and accepted this—children follow in the footsteps of their parents—but the Nisei resented and chafed at the low wages, long hours, and lack of status which jobs in the ethnic community entailed. [1971, 23]

This employment discrimination was a continuation of the anti-Asian feelings which earlier had produced restrictions on immigration (the Gentlemen's Agreement of 1907–8 and the Oriental Exclusion Act of 1924), land ownership (i.e., the alien land laws), and citizenship. Unlike immigrants from European countries, for example, the Issei could not become naturalized citizens no matter how long they had lived in this country.

Nevertheless, despite the weight of discrimination, the Japanese made remarkable progress in economic niches that were open to them. This was the case in California agriculture where they virtually cornered the market in some types of fruits and vegetables (e.g., Iwata 1962). In spite of restrictions on land ownership and leasing, the Issei farmers were able to remain competitive with their white counterparts because of their skill in growing intensive crops, use of unpaid family labor, willingness to cooperate if they had common economic problems, and ability to endure long hours and austere living conditions. Also, as previously noted, some white landowners even defended the Issei sharecroppers and lessees when the alien land laws were being debated as they stood to lose money if they lost their Japanese tenants. They simply could not make as much profit if they farmed the land themselves.

PREWAR ATTITUDES TOWARD DISCRIMINATION

As in any ethnic community, there have always been a variety of reactions among individual Japanese Americans about ways to deal with discrimination as well as more general issues concerning the relationship between the ethnic culture and the majority group culture. In the prewar years, some attempted to deal with these issues by proving that they were "100 percent Americans." This was perhaps best expressed in the positions of the Japanese American Citizens League (JACL), founded in 1930 by a group of better educated and acculturated Nisei just as their generation was coming of age. Their official creed includes the following passage:

> Although some individuals may discriminate against me, I shall never become bitter or lose faith, for I know that such persons are not representative of the majority of the American people. True, I shall do all in my power to discourage such practices, but I shall do it in the American way—above board, in the open, through the courts of law, by education, by proving myself to be worthy of equal treatment and consideration.... Because I believe in America, and I trust she believes in me, and because I have received innumerable benefits from her, I pledge myself to do honor to her at all times and all places; to support her constitution; to obey her laws; to respect her flag; to defend her against all enemies, foreign and domestic; to actively assume my duties and obligations as a citizen, cheerfully and without any reservations whatsoever, in the hope that I may become a better American in a greater America. [Daniels 1971, 24–25]

Over the years, there have been a variety of interpretations of the "meaning" of the accommodating posture just described. From the immediate postwar era through the late 1960s, the dominant view was that the acquiescence of Japanese Americans was a reflection of their cultural tradition (e.g., Hosokowa 1969; Peterson 1970). This interpretation was supported by a good deal of anthropological evidence that in fact Japanese culture does emphasize the idea that a good person should be quiet and unobtrusive in his/her affairs and conform to the group of which s/he is a member (see, e.g., Zander 1983). The idea of "fitting in," then, was certainly consistent with the cultural traditions the immigrants brought with them to the United States. Thus, young Nisei were taught by their immigrant parents, the Japanese churches, and the Japanese language schools to be good Americans and especially not to bring "shame" on their families or on the ethnic community as a whole (Fujimoto 1975; Hosokowa 1969; Peterson 1970).

In recent years, however, many scholars have suggested that the

40

interpretation just described is overly simplified. They have pointed out, for example, that the accommodating behavior of Japanese Americans in the prewar period was perhaps as much a result of lack of choice as it was a reflection of Japanese values. In this regard, the critics point out that the acquiescence of the Japanese immigrants and their children was quite typical of what occurred in other immigrant groups at the time.

There was, for example, not much support for cultural diversity in the United States during the first half of the twentieth century. Indeed, nativist movements, especially in the 1920s, aggressively sought to force the immigrants to give up what were seen as backward old-country ways for what was defined as a superior Anglo-American culture (Hofstadter 1955a; 1955b). Moreover, although political entrepreneurs in European immigrant groups formed political organizations to struggle with native white Anglo-Saxon groups in municipal politics (Banfield and Wilson 1963, 116–127), the vast majority of the children of the European immigrants, like the Nisei, devoted considerable energy to proving that they too were 100 percent Americans. Indeed, as a number of scholars have pointed out, it is only in the financially and psychologically secure third generation of these European ethnic groups that we find any kind of aggressive stance on cultural pluralism (e.g., Handlin 1951; Novak 1972).

Moreover, while not denying the centrality of the value of quiet perseverance in Japanese and Japanese American cultures, scholars have pointed out that there is ample historical evidence that Japanese Americans could adopt a very aggressive stance on occasions when it seemed to be an effective way of pursuing their interests. Around the turn of the century, for example, Issei farm laborers were sometimes characterized as difficult by the growers for whom they worked since they would strike if they thought they were being treated unfairly. At times, the Japanese Association sought legal and political remedies to the laws that discriminated against them (Ichioka 1971; 1977a).

Regardless of what particular interpretation one gives to the prewar behavior of Japanese Americans, however, it is clear that Japanese culture did provide people in the ethnic community with some critical "survival tools" in dealing with a very difficult and often hostile environment. Foremost among these were those principles, noted earlier, for organizing collectively. The long history of creating organizations to deal with collective problems quite naturally led to the development of organizations like the Japanese Association among the Issei and the JACL among the Nisei. Even though the nature and purposes of these two organizations were very different, they both represent collective responses to problems facing members of the ethnic community.

Equally important was the "relativistic" ethic in Japanese culture which said, in effect, that specific cultural beliefs and practices could be altered so long as they strengthened the survival of the community. Thus, Japanese Americans were able to adopt Americanized practices, even in highly sensitive areas like religion, without sacrificing the integrity of the group itself. This gave them a marked advantage over many other immigrant groups which experienced considerable struggle and conflict over whether they should adopt American ways or hold on to the ways of the "old country."

This is not to suggest, of course, that different generations of Japanese did not have their conflicts, in the same fashion as did different generations in other immigrant groups, but rather to point out that Japanese Americans may have had an easier time accommodating to certain kinds of change because of the priority placed on group survival, over and above the preservation of any particular practice or belief. This cultural world view was to become especially central in the Japanese American struggle to adapt to the psychic and economic pain caused by the evacuation and incarceration during World War II.

While, in one sense, the fact that they survived such a horrible set of injustices with remarkable poise is a tribute to their individual and collective courage, it is also a tribute to the resiliency of Japanese and Japanese American cultures. The "structural constraints" with which Japanese Americans had to deal during the war years could hardly have been predicted either by their experience in Japan or even in the United States up to that time. Nonetheless, the kinds of responses which the ethnic community made to these exigencies followed some characteristic Japanese principles. Despite the controversy and conflict within the community, including the forced transfer of power from the immigrant to the second generation, the Japanese American community did stay intact during the war years and emerged in the postwar era a changed but still viable entity.

THE ATTACK ON PEARL HARBOR

In the mid to late 1930s, when Japan was invading other parts of Asia under the banner of the Greater East Asia Coprosperity Sphere, many Issei no doubt felt considerable national pride. They, like older persons of Italian or German origin, were romantically connected with events about whose particulars they were not familiar. Frequently, their perspective was biased from reading pro-Japanese vernacular newspapers (Daniels 1971, 23–24). During the early phases of Japanese imperialism in Asia, some local Japanese Associations sponsored events to provide sundry packages for Japanese soldiers (Spicer 1946).

In the months immediately preceding the attack on Pearl Harbor, however, most Issei and older Nisei became increasingly alarmed, as did other Americans, about the prospects of a conflict between the United States and Japan (Daniels 1971, 26–27). By this time, even the Issei were coming to accept the possibility of conflict and most viewed their position to be on the American side. Weglyn has given us a poignant description of one Issei father's emotional reaction to seeing his son after he had been drafted in 1939:

> When he saw his son standing proudly in a U.S. Army uniform, he knew that he had been wedded to the United States for all these years, even though there had been many in-laws, as it were, who mistreated him. . . . At the moment the Issei were in a frame of mind that would easily have led him to fight the Japanese forces, should they invade the Pacific Coast. Emotionally it would have been an extremely painful thing to do, but he would have done it just the same, for he saw quite clearly that it was the only thing for him to do as one who had been "wedded" to the United States. [1976, 45]

Despite the months of rumors and evidence of a possible outbreak of war between the United States and Japan, Japanese Americans like their fellow countrymen were shocked and confused by the attack on Pearl Harbor. The following are some reactions by Nisei to the news:

> I was in junior college and it [the news about Pearl Harbor] was so shocking. I was so embarrassed, and felt like crawling under the seat when we heard President Roosevelt's announcement in class. I just felt as if we were inferior and part of the enemy at that time. It was a very bad feeling. [Tule Lake Committee 1980, 15]

Another Nisei recalled:

> The day the war broke out, I was at a party for one of my Caucasian friends. I was the only Japanese present at the gathering. It was a sort of luncheon. The radio was turned on and that was the first time I heard of Pearl Harbor and it was such a shock. Everything in the room went blank for me. It's a day I hate to think about now and I hope I never have to live through another day like that. I felt like I wanted the floor to open up and swallow me. I felt like I was sitting on an abyss. I was scared to death. I dreaded the thought of war and the hatred which it would arouse. I felt everybody's eyes on me and I desperately wished that I was in a dark cave alone. The people at the luncheon were very understanding and they immediately comforted me. I felt a sense of guilt for what Japan had done. I was too stunned to even think straight. [Thomas 1952, 491]

Feelings of vulnerability and fear became dominant as the FBI began rounding up 500 Issei leaders who were officially defined as enemy aliens. Most of these persons were merely community leaders in organizations such as the Buddhist temple or Japanese Association. Their funds were impounded and they were shipped off. Their families were not told where they were being sent. Eventually they ended up in separate detention camps run by the Justice Department in the interior of the country. The vernacular press was quickly silenced and travel was restricted for all persons of Japanese ancestry. Many Nisei students dropped out of college, viewing the pursuit of education as pointless. For all practical purposes the ethnic community became immobilized (Saiki 1986).

More than two months passed between the bombing of Pearl Harbor and the issuance of Executive Order 9066, the official act which allowed 110,000 persons of Japanese ancestry living in California, Oregon, Washington, and southern Arizona to be forced into concentration camps. During that time, military and government officials and committees expressed varying arguments for and against internment. Four facts stand out most clearly in historical accounts of this event.

The first is that there never was any real evidence of an actual or potential threat to national security from persons of Japanese ancestry in the United States. There were some Issei and Kibei (second generation born in the U.S. but educated in Japan) who were secretly rooting for Japan, but even the FBI and military intelligence concluded that there was no real danger of a fifth column movement among the Japanese. Curiously, however, the definitive Munson report, which was prepared several months before the attack on Pearl Harbor and found no danger of collaboration between Japanese Americans and the Japanese (in either Hawaii or on the West Coast) was suppressed until after the war (Weglyn 1976, 34).

Moreover, it is clear that even in 1941 and early 1942 the American intelligence community was aware that the Japanese did not have the intention, let alone the capability, to invade the continental U.S. Roger Daniels observes that

> the nearest Japanese aircraft during most of December were attacking Wake Island, more than 5000 miles west of San Francisco, and any major Japanese surface vessels or troops were even farther away. In fact elements of the Luftwaffe over the North Atlantic were actually closer to California than any Japanese planes. California and the West Coast of the continental United States were in no way seriously threatened by the Japanese military. This finding does not represent just the hindsight of the military historian; the high command of the American Army realized it at the time. Official estimates of Japanese capabilities made late in December concluded correctly that a large-scale invasion was beyond the capacity of the Japanese military but that a hit-and-run raid somewhere along the West Coast was possible. [1971, 38]

Within the military, it was those officers who were most involved in combat operations, such as General Stilwell, who were least impressed with the hysteria about a possible invasion of the West Coast. In the case of General Mark Clark, there was specific opposition and revulsion to the thought of a forced evacuation of American citizens. Rather, the most vehement support for the internment policy came from a rather inept officer, General John

L. De Witt, who never saw combat during the entire war but did hold the powerful position of Commander of the Western Defense Region (Daniels 1971, 36–41, 65–66).

Second, long-standing racism and particularly resentment over the economic success of the Japanese in agriculture on the West Coast played a major role in precipitating the evacuation. Many in the mass media, especially the Hearst newspapers, fanned the flames of anti-Japanese sentiment. This was reinforced by public officeholders in California and some federal government officials in Washington, such as Secretary of the Navy Frank Knox.

One of the notable figures involved in these activities was then-California Attorney General Earl Warren, who later was to achieve eminence as a progressive on the U.S. Supreme Court. Warren came to Washington to testify before a Congressional Committee on February 21, 1942. He began his testimony by arguing that there indeed was a clear danger of a fifth column movement on the West Coast. He said:

> Unfortunately . . . . many of our people and some of our authorities and, I am afraid, many of our people in other parts of the country are of the opinion that because we have had no sabotage and no fifth column activities in this State since the beginning of the war, that means that none have been planned for us. But I take the view that that is the most ominous sign in our whole situation. It convinces me more than perhaps any other factor that the sabotage that we are to get, the fifth column activities that we are to get, are timed just like Pearl Harbor was timed and just like the invasion of France, and of Denmark, and of Norway, and all of those other countries. [U.S. Congress Select Committee 1942, 11014–11015]

The racist underpinnings of Warren's argument are perhaps most clearly seen in his reasoning as to why persons of Japanese ancestry born in America posed the most serious threat to national security. He continued:

> in some instances the children of those people [i.e., the Issei] have been sent to Japan for their education, either in whole or in part, and while they are over there they are indoctrinated with the idea of Japanese imperialism. They receive their religious instruction which ties up their religion with their Emperor, and they come back here imbued

with the ideas and the policies of Imperial Japan. While I do not cast a reflection on every Japanese who is born in this country—of course we will have loyal ones—I do say that the consensus of opinion is that taking the groups by and large there is more potential danger to this State from the group that is born here than from the group born in Japan. [U.S. Congress Select Committee 1942, 11014–11015]

Finally, Warren developed a line of reasoning as to why it would not be possible to separate disloyal from loyal Japanese Americans:

We believe that when we are dealing with the Caucasian race we have methods that will test the loyalty of them, and we believe that we can, in dealing with the Germans and the Italians, arrive at some fairly sound conclusions because of our knowledge of the way they live in the community and have lived for many years. But when we deal with the Japanese we are in an entirely different field and we cannot form any opinion that we believe to be sound. Their method of living, their language, make for this difficulty. [U.S. Congress Select Committee 1942, 11011–11015]

The third and perhaps most painful fact is that many persons who might otherwise be considered supporters of civil rights actively called for the incarceration. This included, for example, the liberal columnist Walter Lippmann (Daniels 1971, 68–70) and, of course, the president of the United States, Franklin D. Roosevelt (Daniels 1971, 72; Weglyn 1976, 73–74). Weglyn, quoting William Petersen, goes even further, suggesting that

The stripping of a minority of their constitutional rights, indeed the entire evacuation-internment folly, was "engineered by liberals. . . . Among the civilians one can hardly name a person, from the President down to local officials, who was not one." [1976, 112]

Mayor La Guardia of New York City, who had taken an active role in defense of immigrants, very carefully omitted any reference to persons of Japanese ancestry when he proclaimed the patriotism of persons of German and Italian ancestry (Daniels 1971, 35). The only significant opposition to the internment policy came from the Quakers and the American Civil Liberties Union (ACLU) (Weglyn, 1976, 104–105; Daniels 1971, 141). Even the Communist Party, which had a few Japanese American members among students and labor activists, not only removed them from the Party at the beginning of the war, but also supported the incarceration.

Fourth, the most damaging evidence with respect to any case that one might try to make that the incarceration was simply a hysterical reaction to Pearl Harbor and not motivated by racism or economic self-interest is the fact that with the exception of about one thousand individuals, persons of Japanese ancestry in Hawaii were not sent to camps. If, as General De Witt and others had argued, those of Japanese ancestry posed a threat to security then obviously they would have been more dangerous in Hawaii, where American soil had been actually attacked and where Japanese Americans were much closer to the war zone. Evidence that Hawaii was militarily more critical is provided by the fact that it was placed under martial law on the day it was attacked (Weglyn 1976, 87).

The question of whether the Japanese in Hawaii should be handled in the same manner as on the mainland was actively debated in the government. A critical event in determining the outcome of this debate was the placing of the Islands under martial law. This removed the territory of Hawaii from the control of the Interior Department and placed it in the hands of the Joint Chiefs of Staff (Culley 1984). After reviewing their intelligence units' assessments of the widespread rumors about Japanese American sabotage after the attack on Pearl Harbor, the military authorities became convinced that the Japanese population on the Islands was not a serious threat to security. Back in Washington, however, Secretary of the Navy Knox was "firmly committed to removing not only all 20,000 resident Japanese but also the 98,000 Japanese Americans from the island of Oahu to a concentration camp on another island." Further, "President Roosevelt was greatly intrigued by the Knox plan and suggested that the Japanese population be relocated to an Army internment camp located on Molokai Island." After vigorous debate, a War Department plan recommended that "all Japanese residents of the Hawaiian Islands (both citizens and aliens) be transported to the United States mainland and placed under guard at a concentration camp in such a locality as is most suitable" (Weglyn 1976, 50).

Fortunately, other forces began to work against this plan. The military complained that there was inadequate shipping to handle the mass migration and that Japanese American labor was needed to rebuild the damaged facilities in Hawaii. If the Japanese were removed they would have to be replaced with an equivalent skilled labor force from the mainland. Finally, in July of 1942 the military persuaded the secretaries of war and the navy that U.S. citizens should not be transferred en masse to the mainland for internment. The legal rationale for this decision was the mainland habeas corpus proceedings that the ACLU had used to block the internment of thirteen Hawaiian Nisei (Culley 1984). Specific individuals judged to be dangerous could still be incarcerated. Eventually some 1,037 persons, including 912 citizens, were actually evacuated to the mainland under the control of the War Relocation Authority (WRA).

Culley (1984) observes that there was little local economic and political pressure in Hawaii for the removal of Japanese Americans. They made up 37.3 percent of the population in the Islands in 1940 (157,905 persons); their removal would not only have created insurmountable logistic problems but would perhaps have caused a collapse of the local economy.

Early in 1942, Carl B. Munson, a government worker who previously had studied the mainland Japanese, reported to Congress that the "big bulk" of the first generation Issei were loyal to the U.S. and that among the second generation Nisei approximately 98 percent were loyal. He emphasized their love of Hawaii, noting, "everyone in Hawaii, especially in the dark-skinned laboring classes, places loyalty to Hawaii first, and the United States second. This is not to impugn their loyalty—but they love the Islands" (Munson 1942).

Numerous other reports by Army, Navy, and British intelligence as well as the FBI reached similar conclusions. Another factor which reduced the pressure to incarcerate the Island Japanese was the fact that they were much better integrated into the local social and political fabric. Not only did the majority of the populace have Japanese friends and neighbors, but the Japanese had some political power. On Kauai, for example, four of the seven candidates for district supervisor, including the incumbent, were Japanese

Americans. Although they eventually withdrew to dispel any fear that the Island would be subjugated by Japanese, it illustrates the more favorable position of Hawaiian Japanese vis-à-vis their isolated and almost totally powerless mainland counterparts (Ogawa 1978, 279–280).

This is not to say that Hawaii was a benign environment for Japanese Americans during the war. They had to endure occasional attacks questioning their loyalty, and were constantly forced to go the extra mile to disavow any potential sympathies toward Japan. This is illustrated by an article written for the large Nisei student body in the McKinley High School *Daily Pinion*: "You might as well admit it now that you are on the spot. There is nothing to be gained by fooling oneself at a time like this. Harm is apt to come from being indifferent. The outside world wonders about you" (quoted in the *Honolulu Advertiser*, 1942).

As on the mainland, Japanese Americans closed language schools and Buddhist temples and buried or otherwise destroyed treasured family artifacts such as samurai swords, Japanese flags, and photographs of vacations in Japan. Speak English campaigns were started for the Issei, and Nisei were discouraged from speaking Japanese unless it was absolutely necessary (Ogawa 1978, 315–316). Further, there was uneasiness about how some other ethnic groups would react to the Japanese. In particular, there was tension between the Filipino and Japanese communities because of Japan's military actions in the Philippines.

In response to wartime pressures, the National Association of Buddhist Ministries changed its name, first informally in 1942 and then formally in 1944, to the Buddhist Churches of America. They also dropped the traditional Buddhist symbol, which resembled the Nazi swastika, and replaced it with the eight-spoked Wheel of Law (Kashima 1977, 52, 59, 114).

Nevertheless, a telling indicator of the impact of the differences in treatment of the Japanese in Hawaii compared to that administered on the mainland is the reaction to the call for volunteers to form the all-Japanese 442nd Regimental Combat Team. Only 1,181 volunteers came forward from the ten relocation centers on the mainland while 9,507 volunteered from Hawaii. Initially, the mainland quota was set at 3,000 while the Hawaiian quota was set at

1,500. Eventually, 2,600 from the Islands were sent to join the trainees from the mainland (Ogawa 1978, 332; Weglyn 1976, 143–144, 306).

Immigrant workers arriving in Hawaii. (Photo courtesy Hawaii State Archives.)

Japanese Togo Employment Agency, Seattle, circa 1919. (Photo courtesy Nippon Kan Heritage Association Photo Exhibit Collection, Seattle.)

Sugar workers in Hawaii. (Photo courtesy Hawaii State Archives.)

Japanese families in strawberry field. (Photo courtesy Tom Murakami Collection, Japanese American National Museum Photo Archive.)

Japanese fruit stand. (Photo courtesy Kathleen Yamazaki Collection, Japanese American National Museum Photo Archive.)

Kumamoto Picnic play, 1923. (Photo courtesy Toy Kanegai Collection, Japanese American National Museum Photo Archive.)

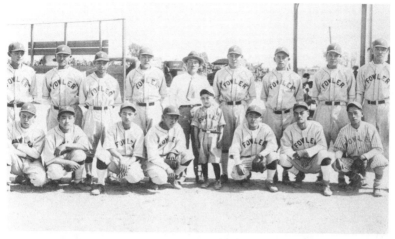

Fowler, California, baseball team, 1925. (Photo courtesy Yoshio Honda Collection, Japanese American National Museum Photo Archive.)

Ansel Adams photo of Kuichiro Nishi's garden, Merritt Park in Manzanar Relocation Center, 1943. (Photo courtesy Kuichiro Nishi family, Japanese American National Museum Photo Archive.)

Man and child in front of a Jerome, Arkansas, Relocation Center guard tower, 1943. (Photo courtesy Arthur S. Fujikawa Collection, Japanese American National Museum Photo Archive.)

The Atomettes, West Los Angeles United Methodist Church girls' club, 1952. (Photo courtesy Mary Ishizuka Collection, Japanese American National Museum Photo Archive.)

Fred Hirasuna (left) and Min Omata among strawberries in their post-war packing shed. (Photo courtesy Fred Hirasuna Collection, Japanese American National Museum Photo Archive.)

Akio Suyematsu, last Japanese American commercial berry farmer on Bainbridge Island, 1988. (Photo courtesy *Bremerton Sun*.)

THREE

THE CONCENTRATION
CAMP EXPERIENCE

 Events on the mainland culminated in the issuance of Executive Order 9066, giving the Secretary of War the authority to designate certain zones "military areas" and to remove "any or all persons" from those areas (Wilson and Hosokawa 1980, 203). Public Proclamation No. 1 designated the western halves of Washington, Oregon, and California as well as the southern part of Arizona as Military Area No. 1. All persons of Japanese ancestry were to be excluded from this area. The proclamation further advised those of Japanese ancestry to move to the interior of the U.S. In response to this, some Japanese Americans hastily relocated out of the defense zone, only to be met by hostility in the communities they entered. Three weeks later, amid considerable confusion, General De Witt issued Public Proclamation No. 4 which forbade further movement from Military Area No. 1. This set up the final conditions for sending thousands of men, women, and children to American concentration camps (e.g., Broom and Kitsuse 1956, 14–15).

The initial authority for administering the evacuation of Japanese Americans was given to the Army, which then created the Wartime Civil Control Administration (WCCA). Since time was needed to build permanent centers, temporary assembly centers were established at fairgrounds (e.g., Fresno County Fairgrounds) and race tracks (e.g., Tanforan and Santa Anita) near Japanese population centers. The Japanese were kept in sixteen of these holding areas until the more permanent "relocation" centers in the interior of the country could be constructed. This phase was completed by August, 1942.

The most obvious cost of the evacuation for Japanese Americans was economic. Given the short time they had to get ready for travel, many families were forced to sell their material goods for a mere fraction of their value. Weglyn notes that

> bargain hunters and junk dealers descended in hordes. The frightened and confused became easy prey to swindlers who threatened to "arrange" for the confiscation of their property if they would not agree to a forced sale. . . . Some permitted hopefully trustworthy white friends to move into their homes as overseers—often rent-free—or to take over the care of their land. . . . There were many who turned over possessions for storage in local Japanese temples and churches, others who simply boarded them up in garages or vacant sheds belonging to kindly disposed neighbors. But pilfering and vandalism often began before they were hardly out of their homes. A postwar survey was to reveal that 80 percent of goods privately stored were "rifled, stolen, or sold during absence." [1976, 77]

By and large, considering the size of the group and the circumstances, the initial movement of Japanese Americans from their homes to the temporary assembly centers went remarkably smoothly. There were nonetheless numerous instances of strife, both between the authorities and the internees and among the internees themselves. Some ended up in rioting. One such incident was the Santa Anita racetrack riot, which is described by sociologist Harry Kitano, himself an evacuee:

> At the Santa Anita Assembly Center, a riot began in response to rumors that a group of evacuee policemen was illegally confiscating electrical appliances and other material for personal use. During this direct confrontation between those interned and those representing the United States Government, there were cries of "Ko-ro-se!" (Kill them!) and "Inu!" (Dog!). A crowd of around 2,000 Japanese, including large numbers of teen-agers, ran aimlessly and wildly about, rumors flew, property was destroyed, and finally an accused policeman was set upon during a routine inspection and badly beaten. The incident was controlled through the intervention of 200 Army MPs, installation of martial law, and stricter security. [1976, 73]

A civilian agency, the War Relocation Authority (WRA), was created to permanently administer the evacuation program. This agency eventually ran ten concentration camps, euphemistically called projects, located on desolate federal land in Arkansas, Arizona, California, Colorado, Idaho, Wyoming, and Utah. The shock Japanese Americans felt when they first saw the camps is described by a Nisei:

> I'll never forget the sad expression on my mother's face when she first set her eyes upon the barren tar-papered barracks, the bare pot-bellied stove—which was to be our home for who knows how long. She tried her best to hold us together as a family. [Tule Lake Committee 1980, 24]

At the height of the incarceration program, each camp contained a population ranging in size from 8,000 to 20,000 individuals.

During the latter half of 1942, the internees were moved from the local assembly centers on the fairgrounds and race tracks to these hastily constructed "permanent" camps. The actual housing consisted of tarpaper barracks built by then-small companies such as Del E. Webb which made enormous profits working on these cost-plus government projects. Not surprisingly, the WRA authorities attempted to place the more Americanized and English speaking Nisei in positions of responsibility. Young people, often in their early twenties, had authority over middle-aged Issei who, until recently, had been the decision makers in the Japanese community. This stripping away of their traditional authority contributed to the demoralization of the Issei. Not only had they lost most of the possessions they had struggled so hard to obtain, but they were incarcerated in an alien subsociety where their authority was transferred to their children (Embree 1943; Spickard 1983). The arrangement caused a great deal of turmoil in the early days of internment. Eventually, in order to reduce conflict, the Issei were given a greater role in formally representing the community to the white administrators (Spicer 1946).

The barracks' living arrangements made it difficult to socialize children in the traditional Japanese way. The Issei could not be too stern with wayward offspring lest their voices carry through the thin walls and disturb their neighbors. The Nisei children, for their part, often ate with their peers in the mess hall and roamed around the camp in packs, thus further escaping the influence of their elders (Kitano 1976, 73–77). Juvenile delinquency became a significant problem in the Japanese American community for the first time (Spicer 1946).

An indication of the demoralization of the Issei was their lack of desire to leave the camps. In 1943, for example, the majority of the Nisei wanted to reestablish their lives outside of the camps but the majority of the Issei preferred to remain within the harsh but secure boundaries of the camps rather than face the uncertainties of life on the outside (Embree 1943; Yatsuhiro, Ishino, and Matsumoto 1944).

By the fall of 1942, the WRA authorities were beginning to think that the sooner the internees could rejoin the mainstream of American life, the better. They had noticed signs of institutionalization and wanted to prevent it from going any further. However, rumors about the hostility of the American public on the outside were constantly circulating among the internees. In addition, they could not return to their former homes on the West Coast. Only the Midwest and East were open to them. Thus, many felt it was wiser to simply sit out the war until they could safely return to the Pacific Coast.

The internees had been told by the WRA that their stay was for the duration of the war. Most were not eager to move yet a third time. Hence, the WRA could not push too hard for resettlement to the East and Midwest without meeting resistance from substantial numbers of internees.

Several observers have claimed that the Buddhist Church has frequently served as a rallying point for Japanese Americans to resist cultural hegemony and discrimination, particularly during World War II (e.g., Okihiro 1984). Ogura in his study of the Gardena Buddhist Church in Southern California suggests that involvement surged in response to discrimination:

> After the passage of the Immigration Law of 1924 discriminating against the Japanese, the number of Buddhists increased rapidly, and so did that of the Buddhist churches. Before that event, some of them had been hesitant in declaring themselves Buddhists, considering such an act impudent in a Christian country. But the immigration law

made them more defiant and bold in asserting what they believed to be their rights, it made them realize the necessity of cooperation for the sake of their own security and welfare, and naturally they sought the centers of their communal activity in their Buddhist churches. [1932, 85–86]

Buddhism was always viewed by the American public as an alien religion. With the outbreak of World War II, those who were Buddhists were more likely to be seen as pro-Japanese. Within days after the attack on Pearl Harbor, Shinto and Buddhist priests were interned in Department of Justice detention camps. Among Japanese Americans themselves, being Christian was seen as being more acculturated. Thus, under the initial pressure of war hysteria, many individuals not only played down their Buddhist beliefs but some even became Christians (Kashima 1977, 54). Even today some Nisei Buddhists feel they were more courageous than their Christian counterparts because they stuck with their disparaged religion through some very trying times.

RESPONSES TO EVACUATION AND INCARCERATION

The picture presented in many journalistic accounts, and oftentimes promoted by organizations such as the JACL, is that despite being persecuted and herded into desolate concentration camps, the internees remained unwavering in their commitment to their country. While there is much truth to this picture it is, as one might expect, oversimplified. There were, in fact, a variety of responses.

From the time of the internment in 1942, persons of Japanese ancestry were legally prevented from serving in the military or working in defense plants. Major exceptions to this rule, however, were individuals who performed a variety of critical military intelligence functions in far-flung corners of the Pacific. This segment of the Japanese American story has only recently received significant attention. During the war, these individuals were forbidden to discuss their work for fear of losing an important advantage over the enemy. Thus, most Americans were unaware of the contributions of Japanese Americans to the war in the Pacific theater. There is no doubt, however, about the important part these 5,000 men played in the war effort. General Charles Willoughby, Chief of

Intelligence for Douglas MacArthur, stated that "the Nisei saved a million lives and shortened the war by two years" (Nakatsu 1988, 79).

Ironically, the story of Japanese American work in military intelligence during the war had its beginnings at the Presidio of San Francisco, which was also the headquarters of General De Witt, one of those most responsible for promoting the incarceration. By 1941, as conflict with Japan became more likely, some in the Army felt it was necessary to have individuals who were proficient in Japanese. Among those holding this view was Captain Kai Rasmussen who was given the responsibility for developing this capability. Authorized to spend a mere $2,000, he was allocated an abandoned hangar at Crissey Field in the Presidio by the Golden Gate. Forty-five Nisei and Kibei along with fifteen others of various extractions were assembled for the first class on November 1, 1941.

After the mass evacuation of Japanese Americans from the Pacific Coast, the Japanese Language School was moved from the Presidio to the more hospitable area of Camp Savage, Minnesota, and renamed the Military Intelligence Service Language School (MISLS). Most of the students were recruited from the concentration camps, sometimes under considerable sanctions from other internees or even family members. Later, others were reassigned from other army units. One of the first persons Rasmussen recruited was John Aiso, a Harvard-trained lawyer who had been drafted earlier but was assigned to a truck repair facility at Camp Hahn near Riverside, California (Yano 1988). Aiso was soon made Director of Academic Training and, after the Battle of Midway when it became possible for Japanese Americans to be commissioned officers, was directly commissioned with the rank of Major. After the war, John Aiso was to become the first Japanese American judge.

The graduates of the school became the "eyes and ears" of the Allied Forces in the Pacific. Assigned in teams, they translated captured documents and messages, analyzed features of downed enemy aircraft, interrogated prisoners, broadcast propaganda, encouraged Japanese soldiers and civilians to surrender, helped prepare the instruments of surrender, worked on various aspects of the War Crimes trials, and were an important element of the occupation forces. MISLS graduates were at Guadalcanal, with

Merrill's Marauders in Burma, Corregidor, Mindanao, the Solomons, the Marianas, Kwajalein, Leyte, New Guinea, Luzon, Iwo Jima, Okinawa, and numerous other major battles.

These men sometimes were mistaken for the enemy by American or other Allied troops, such as the Chinese and Australians. A Sergeant Hachiya, for example, who parachuted behind enemy lines in the Philippines was killed by an American soldier who mistook him for an infiltrating Japanese soldier (Yano 1988). What is most tragic, however, is that while these Nisei and Kibei linguists fought soldiers from the land of their parents, many of their own family and friends were locked up in concentration camps.

In the middle of 1942, the Army changed its policy of not assigning Nisei to combat roles. The decision was made to form an all-Japanese volunteer combat unit to fight in Europe. First the Hawaiian Provisional Battalion, part of the National Guard, was activated as the 100th Infantry Battalion. Soon afterwards this change of policy was extended to those incarcerated on the mainland.

In the camps, the change in policy met with considerable controversy, particularly the restriction about volunteering for a segregated, all-Japanese unit. Many felt resentment about being treated differently yet another time. The many enthusiastic volunteers from Hawaii and the much smaller number from the mainland camps formed the highly decorated all-Japanese American units, the 100th Battalion and the 442nd Regimental Combat Team. By the end of the war, they had received more than 18,000 individual and unit awards, including a Medal of Honor. Because of its heavy losses, the 100th Battalion came to be known as the "Purple Heart Battalion." The motto of the 442nd Regimental Combat Team was "Go for Broke." This is a Hawaiian pidgin phrase from the world of poker games and craps. It means to "shoot the works" on the deal of a single card or one throw of the dice.

Several points about the wartime record of the Nisei soldiers are worth mentioning. First, there is no doubt about their outstanding performance. Some writers have emphasized that various interests wanted to publicize the Nisei military record to increase their public acceptance when they returned to the mainstream of American life. The Nisei volunteers themselves saw it as their opportunity and obligation to prove their Americanism with blood. Dennis Ogawa, describing the feelings of those in Hawaii, writes:

> On March 28, 1943, thousands of these Nisei inductees, ready to be sent to Camp Shelby, Mississippi, to become part of the 442nd Regimental Combat Team, gathered on the grounds of Iolani Palace. Leis, tearful farewells, and gifts filled the occasion as one of the largest gatherings of people in Honolulu witnessed the *aloha* ceremonies which took place that day. A superpatriotic aura surrounded the whole proceedings, for the press, the island community, and the Japanese community viewed these Nisei soldiers as the vindicators of loyalty and Americanism of the Japanese of Hawaii. [1978, 322]

There is no question that the superlative war record of the Nisei was a critical element in the postwar acceptance of Japanese Americans. In fact, it is doubtful whether the Civil Liberties Act of 1988, the redress bill for those incarcerated, would have passed without it. There were, however, other responses to the imprisonment of Japanese Americans. Proponents of these positions were oftentimes equally adamant in their belief that they were pursuing a just cause and indeed were following traditional American approaches to injustice.

One such response was an organized draft resistance movement, started in the Heart Mountain Wyoming Center, which called itself the Fair Play Committee (FPC). This movement began after the start of registration of Japanese Americans for the draft and immediately preceding the institution of the draft itself, in January of 1944. After the draft became a reality, the FPC began holding meetings and publishing bulletins. They argued that not to resist the denial of their Constitutional rights was to be disloyal to American democracy and its traditions (Daniels 1988, 270–271).

Several of the FPC leaders were summarily sent to the center that had been turned into a segregation camp, Tule Lake. Eventually, 63 men refused induction and a mass trial was held in Federal District Court in Cheyenne. After a two-week trial, they were found guilty and sentenced to three years in federal prison. More young men continued to refuse induction until a total of approximately 120 were charged with draft evasion. Eighty-five from Heart Mountain and 267 altogether from all of the camps were convicted of evading the draft. The ACLU refused to represent the draft resisters, saying that they "had a strong moral case but a very weak legal one."

The seven leaders of the FPC, most of whom were not subject to the draft, were indicted and arrested in July 1944. Their case, after being tried in district court, resulted in a four year sentence. They were sent to Fort Leavenworth Federal Prison where they served eighteen months, until the appellate court reversed the decision. In 1947 President Truman pardoned all of the resisters (Emi 1986).

Some Nisei and Kibei also were assigned to what became the 1800 Engineer Service Battalion. This unit was manned by soldiers of German, Italian and Japanese descent over whom the Army wanted to keep close watch. Japanese Americans who were assigned to this unit were there because of their reactions to racial incidents in the service or the incarceration. A typical story is that of a soldier who was training for the MIS at Camp Savage. His father was in the Lordsburg Internment Camp and his mother was incarcerated at the Manzanar Relocation Center. He wrote the Enemy Alien Control Unit in Washington requesting that his father be allowed to join his mother:

> Both were behind barbed wire, I wrote, so would it endanger the security of the United States if they could be together? Nothing came of this and other pleas I had made to him and other authorities. When the infamous questionnaire [see below] was distributed to every student at the intelligence school, I answered no/yes, but with "no" qualified with a letter of explanation.
>
> But just before my graduation, my request for a furlough to visit my mother in Manzanar was denied because no Nisei were allowed into the Western Defense Zone. It seemed incongruous to be preparing for a dangerous and highly secretive mission for the U.S. Army, while being forbidden to make farewell visits to family and friends in camp in California. This ridiculous military order was later rescinded, but only after I had blown my stack to the wrong people at Camp Savage. As a result I, along with approximately 18 others who had complained about the situation of their families, was ousted from the school, eventually demoted to the rank of private, and transferred to the 1800 for bearing "an attitude which is considered undesirable in a first class soldier of the Army of the United States." [Shimo 1986]

At the same time that the Army started seeking volunteers for the 442nd, the WRA began actively encouraging Nisei to resettle permanently outside of the camps in order to reduce the possibility of losing their initiative and becoming dependent and to help alleviate labor shortages in the Midwest and East. In order to implement both of these policy changes, the authorities decided that they needed more specific criteria for determining the loyalty of individual Japanese Americans. Ironically, the resulting program was in fact a return, in principle at least, to the more narrow view of loyalty risks which many of the military decision makers argued for at the outbreak of the war. Although it can be seen as a loosening up of restrictions on the imprisoned population, it also had many disturbing effects, such as fostering divisions between generations and family members and causing rumors and anxiety in general to increase (e.g., Arensberg 1942).

The program, jointly administered by the Army and the WRA, was called registration. Its key element was a questionnaire designed to "separate the loyal from the disloyal." It was titled "Application for Leave Clearance." Its absurdity is succinctly captured by Bosworth:

> In retrospect, the entire registration program appears to have been a sophomoric and half-baked idea, if not indeed a stupid and costly blunder. In the long run, nothing could have been more certain or more simple than this: If there had been any actual Japanese agents or spies in the Relocation Centers, in February, 1943, they would have been the very first to profess their loyalty on paper, so that they could carry on their work. [1967, 168]

All internees, Issei and Nisei, men and women, were asked a series of questions, the two critical ones being numbers 27 and 28. In the male version, individuals were asked: "Are you willing to serve in the armed forces of the United States on combat duty, wherever ordered?" and "Will you swear unqualified allegiance to the United States of America and faithfully defend the United States from any or all attack by foreign or domestic forces, and forswear any allegiance or obedience to the Japanese emperor or to any other foreign government, power or organization?" (Thomas and Nishimoto 1946, 57–58).

Given their previous treatment and not knowing what the government intended to do with their responses to the questionnaire, many of the internees were understandably apprehensive. Further, the questions made no sense to the Issei. At their age, should they be willing to volunteer for combat? Moreover, since the Issei could not become U.S. citizens, by forswearing allegiance to Japan, they would become men without a country. Eventually, the question relevant to the latter issue was rewritten for the Issei. It asked whether they would swear to abide by U.S. law and not interfere with the war effort. For women, question 27 asked whether they would volunteer for the Army Nurse Corps or the WACs.

Conflicting interpretations of the authorities' motives as well as different opinions about the utility of different responses were found between and within generations and families. Adding to the general confusion and fear surrounding the "loyalty" test was the fact that the Army and the WRA devoted very little effort to explaining their rationale for the questionnaire and what might be the likely effects on families which answered "yes-yes" as opposed to "no-no" on questions 27 and 28. Thus, many responses had nothing to do with loyalty at all. They could be, for example, a way of showing resistance to being "pushed around again," or they could be attempts to avoid the military or to keep the family together (e.g., Spicer 1946). Others answered the questions negatively in order to avoid what they saw as the possibility of being forced to resettle outside in hostile white communities (Thomas and Nishimoto 1946, 88).

One of the complications presented by the loyalty questions was that the Issei and Nisei had very different fears and aspirations with respect to leaving the camps. Most Issei were reluctant to begin an uncertain future outside of the camps, isolated from other Japanese. They believed that their ties with fellow ethnics were crucial for their economic livelihood. Some Nisei, on the other hand, viewed the loyalty questions as an opportunity either to enter the Army and prove their loyalty or, more frequently, simply as a means of getting out of the centers and moving to the Midwest or East, to reenter the labor market and get on with their lives.

The two "loyalty questions" often caused a great deal of individual anxiety and guilt as well as strife within the family. A person's response was seen not only as impacting on him/her but also on other family members as well. Many Nisei deeply felt that a "no-no" response was not only a personal disgrace but reflected badly on all Japanese Americans. Some Issei, on the other hand, reasoned that if members of the family gave "no-no" responses, it would keep the family together and prevent their sons from being taken away by the Army. This was very important to them, as their older sons were a major resource for dealing with the world outside of the immediate Japanese community. Some representative Nisei views were:

> The Japanese people felt that they had been pushed around and evacuated and it was silly to ask the Nisei to go volunteer after all that. . . . If they had just asked the Japanese people to take a vote for this country without the evacuation and all those things coming afterwards, I think that 90 per cent of them would have said "yes." It was too late to ask them about loyalty to this country when they had already said that they did not want the Japanese in California because they distrusted them. [Thomas 1952, 354]

> Most of my friends answered "yes-yes." We didn't discuss the thing too much as we were old enough to know what was the only course for us to take. There was no use in trying to show our discouraged feelings by answering "no" because that would not have gotten us any place. We wanted to be loyal to this country, but it often looked like the odds were against us and we were distrusted too much. I answered "double yes" myself as I felt that if I didn't I would be shipped out to Japan. I knew that I had nothing to do with the old country and I had no business there. There wasn't anything else for me [to do]. [Thomas 1952, 355]

> There were a lot of us who resisted. At the same time, the Army came in and they had a Nisei representative recruiting volunteers so we thought it was one and the same thing. There were so many questions, "What happens if . . . ?" There was great confusion. We went around to see what others were doing. For the family, the decision was very unanimous. My mother's first concern was to keep the family together. Her great fear was that if we registered, we would be drafted and sent to the Army. If my father had been with us, I think we might have registered. [Tule Lake Committee 1980, 28]

Tragically, some Nisei children who did not give positive answers to the questionnaire were subsequently sent to Tule Lake,

71

and eventually Japan, solely because of their parents' position. In the end, approximately 11 percent, or 7,600 persons, in the camps gave negative responses to the so-called loyalty questions. They were derisively labeled "no-no's" by the other internees and 6,700 of them were moved to Tule Lake, which was designated as a segregation camp for repatriates, expatriates, and other "disloyals." At Tule Lake, many "yes-yes's" were harassed as *inus* (dogs). The "yes-yes" people in this camp were to be moved to one of the nine other projects although many, weary of yet another move, stayed at Tule Lake. This camp was selected as the segregation camp as it had the largest number of persons who answered no to question 28 or refused to register. There were large variations from camp to camp in both registration and volunteering for military service. Thomas and Nishimoto (1946) point out that the competency of the various local WRA administrators, along with the background characteristics of the individuals in a particular camp, strongly affected how internees responded to registration and segregation. Tule Lake had a particularly troublesome history in this regard.

Once Tule Lake was designated a segregation camp, it became the site of a great deal of turmoil. Many new "no-no's" were mixed in with those "yes-yes's" who did not want to move. Two largely Kibei (born in the United States but educated in Japan) pro-Japanese groups, the Sokuji Kikoku Hoshi-dan (Organization to Serve the Mother Country) and the Hokoku Seinen-dan (Young Men's Organization to Serve the Mother Country) promoted activities irritating and worrisome to WRA authorities, who were attempting to present the most positive image to the American public in preparation for emptying the camps. Their trademarks were sweatshirts emblazoned with the rising sun (symbol of the Japanese empire) and the "bozu" haircut (a sign of defiance). They made every effort to give the appearance of a quasi-military group, performing calisthenics and marching on the camp athletic fields in the early morning hours. Members of the two organizations intimidated other camp inmates into joining them. By the fall of 1944, almost a thousand young men belonged to the Sokuji Kikoku Hoshi-dan and the Hokoku Seinen-dan (Christgau 1985).

The WRA would have preferred to move the members of the Sokuji Kikoku Hoshi-dan and the Hokoku Seinen-dan to the Department of Justice enemy alien camps so that they could strengthen their case that Tule Lake and the nine other WRA camps were filled with loyal Americans who should be released. Because the members of the quasi-military groups were American citizens, however, they could not, by law, be placed in the camps for aliens (Ennis 1981).

The "solution" to the problem of dealing with the disruptive internees was to amend the Nationality Act of 1940, making it possible for United States citizens to renounce their citizenship. When Congress passed the amended legislation, a few hundred applications, mostly from Hokoku leaders, were submitted from Tule Lake (Christgau 1985).

In December of 1944 when the ban on persons of Japanese ancestry returning to the West Coast was lifted, rumors ran rampant in Tule Lake that the Nisei would be split from their Issei parents who would be deported or that the families would be forced to relocate to hostile white communities. The Hokoku argued that renouncing one's citizenship would be the safest way to ensure that families would be kept together in the camps. When the Army hearing officers asked whether the internees wanted to "go out" or renounce their citizenship, over 2,000 applied for renunciation. Soon this number swelled to over 5,000. Although the Hokoku were a small percentage of the total population of segregated Japanese Americans, they were successful in pressuring a substantial number of non-member Nisei in Tule Lake to sign forms renouncing their citizenship.

When the war ended, President Truman signed an executive order which made the so-called "renunciants" subject to removal to Japan. Thus, many of these persons were forced into the very situation which the Hokoku had convinced them they could avoid. Faced with deportation, many renunciants protested that their decisions had been made in the face of misinformation and coercion. Nonetheless, only 2,280 were granted exemptions from deportation while 7,100 were shipped to Japan.

As these events started to unfold, a feisty, persistent, and committed white attorney, Wayne Collins, concluded that renunciation under detention was unconstitutional. In 1948, he successfully argued before the courts that the deportation order should be overturned because the renunciations were the result of government and Hokoku "duress, menace, coercion, and intimidation" (Christgau 1985).

As a result of this legal change and the extremely difficult conditions in postwar Japan, the vast majority of the renunciants eventually had their citizenship restored and returned to the U.S. However, except for the 1,004 children who were held to have unconstitutionally renounced their citizenship, Collins had to *individually* process affidavits for the remaining 3,300 adults. The last case was not completely processed until March of 1968 (Christgau, 1985).

EFFECTS OF THE INCARCERATION EXPERIENCE

Although it will never be possible fully to measure the effects of the evacuation, incarceration, and relocation on Japanese Americans, some facts are incontrovertible. The most obvious is that many suffered catastrophic economic losses. The Commission on Wartime Relocation and Internment of Civilians estimated that the total loss suffered by Japanese Americans was between $1.2 and $3.1 billion (Taylor 1986). The Evacuation Claims Act of 1948 eventually disbursed a mere $38 million, the last payment of which was made in 1965 (Daniels 1971, 168–169).

Perhaps even more significant than the direct dollar losses was the destruction of the economic infrastructure, especially in agriculture, which the Issei had worked so hard to develop. While much of the nation was experiencing a booming war economy, Japanese Americans not only lost the opportunities for growth which occurred during those years but, in many instances, their shops, farms, packing sheds, and fishing boats. Some of these industries were reestablished on a smaller scale after the war. Others, such as the fishing business, virtually disappeared (Bloom and Reimer 1949, 32–68, 158–159).

The wartime experience also radically altered the relationship of the Japanese community to mainstream American society in a more general way. Before the war, the ethnic community was quite isolated from the larger society, separated in part by racism but also by a strong patriarchal Issei power structure. The relocation, incarceration, and resettlement process dramatically weakened the authority of the Issei. Not only did they lose their economic niche, but their power within the Japanese community was eroded as well. When the Nisei, who had become the major decision makers in the community, had the opportunity to pick up the threads of their lives, most of them attempted to seize the emerging economic opportunities in the larger society. The WRA's policy of encouraging the internees to disperse geographically during resettlement to minimize hostility further encouraged the assimilation of Japanese Americans into mainstream society.

Since virtually all mainland Nisei and Issei have experienced the incarceration, it acts as a shared symbolic bond. The change in their life course was so dramatic that most Nisei divide their lives into two distinct periods, "before camp" and "after camp." Moreover, the camp experience remains meaningful to the Sansei, even though they were very young or not even born at the time, as evidenced by their strong involvement and support for the redress effort and their pilgrimages to former camp sites. Even after forty years, "camp" is a shared symbol which ties together the Japanese American community and increases group cohesiveness.

The psychological sequelae and life course trajectory effects of the camp experience are difficult to document empirically because they are confounded with so many other historical and developmental changes in the lives of those involved. Nevertheless, the stress from the long periods of uncertainty, separation from family members, economic losses, and stigmatization have left their marks. The most tragic victims were the Issei. Not only were many too old to start their economic struggle from scratch all over again, but the subsociety they had created, which provided meaning and security in their lives, was destroyed. The ethnic community was rebuilt in the postwar years but the Issei never regained their position of authority in it.

Among the Nisei, the incarceration created a degree of cynicism and distrust of government that persist to this day. Evidence of the initial impact of the incarceration comes from the fact that fewer than 1,200 of the over 10,000 persons who volunteered for the all-Japanese 442nd Regimental Combat Team and the 100th Infantry Battalion came from the mainland camps while the rest of the volunteers came from Hawaii where the Japanese were not interned. Many Nisei became much more aware of their unique relationship to American society as a result of the camp experience.

A relatively small minority remain very bitter. These are usually persons who suffered catastrophic economic losses.

On the other hand, discussions with Nisei today who were teenagers or in their early twenties during incarceration often elicit statements about how much fun they had in camp. In fact, many younger persons did experience many aspects of a "good time" during camp. Not only did they get out from under the tight control of their conservative parents but they no longer had to work long hours on the family farm or shop. Age graded cliques roamed the camps. The average age of the incoming Nisei was seventeen. This meant that the Nisei were entering the prime dating age. In a typical camp of 10,000 there were many peers of both sexes available. It was only natural for many of these Nisei to associate the constant round of dances and other social events which were quickly organized with a "good time." Although not frequently mentioned, there are reports of considerable sexual activity in firebreaks and empty barracks after these social events (e.g., Thomas 1952, 286).

At the same time, however, it is likely that what many Nisei report about camp life is a classic case of selective recall. Their verbalizations may be understood as an attempt to minimize reliving the pain and humiliation associated with certain wartime experiences. The late Edison Uno, for example, described being sent to camp as similar to being raped. Ng (1989) suggests some parallels with being an incest victim. Even though one knows he or she was wronged, there is also the feeling of degradation which makes it difficult to talk about the experience. Discussing the incarceration with non-Japanese not only may bring about an insensitive response but, in a sense, stigmatizes the group again and points out a gulf which most Nisei have been attempting to bridge much of their lives. Thus, painful memories tend to be minimized while those that are humorous, entertaining, or otherwise have high interest value are repeatedly bantered about. An important consequence of the contemporary redress movement which we will discuss in the next section is that, for many Nisei, it helped purge some of the repressed feelings associated with the incarceration.

Wendy Ng, who interviewed Sansei about their feelings about the incarceration and their parents' discussion of it, reports that typically they had to piece together bits of stories and fragmented behaviors to get a picture of their parents' experience. Usually, it was spoken about only among family and Japanese friends. One of the women she interviewed described how her father would deal with the incarceration experience:

> He would never talk about it unless he felt safe. There were a couple of times when I had, I remember one guy I was dating, who was white. He was asking Dad about it and it was . . . I got really uncomfortable because it was quite clear that Dad didn't feel comfortable talking to him about it because the guy was being insensitive and ignorant. [1989, 8]

Another Sansei woman described her father's handling of the camp experience in the following way:

> Well, he always referred to it as camp . . . "back when we were in camp," and sometimes he would tell funny stories. And sometimes not. He never talked much about how he felt. We just sort of got that out of the way he talked about it. [1989, 7]

The following quotes from a Sansei woman describe the fragmented behaviors that they have had to rely upon to get some feeling for the meaning of the internment for their parents.

> My dad would sort of drop these hints. Very subtle things like, he'd say, like, you know how you get those, sometimes those terrible gift packs where, for Christmas, like Knotts Berry Farms jelly and stuff. One of them was orange marmalade. And he refused to eat any of it. Just refused. He said, "I just don't like it. I refuse to eat it." And we'd just go, "How? How could you, we never saw you eat this before?"
> And my mom never made any before. She'd make jams and things, but, how do you know if you don't like it? Then he said, "Well, in camp they made us eat this every single day for breakfast, that's all they had, every single day." And he just goes, "And I can't even look at it. I can't stand the smell of it."
> He would say stuff like that and we'd get the message that it was really something unpleasant. It etched an unpleasant memory in him that he wouldn't go as far as to eat it now, even though he's in his sixties, he wouldn't act on some of that.

From her mother, the same Sansei observed the following:

> My mom had this necklace of tiny-like shells and it was really crudely
> made. But they were these little teeny-tiny shells. They were from Tule
> Lake. She and her girl friends had collected up these little shells and
> strung them in necklaces. And she never wore it, you know. It was in
> her drawer . . . she had it in the bottom of her jewelry box and she
> never wore it. She never took it out. It's really delicate. And so, we
> kind of got the story from her on that. [1989, 8]

Nevertheless, perhaps the most striking thing about the effects
of the evacuation and incarceration is the fact that individual
Japanese Americans and their ethnic community survived as well
as they did. Studies of the effects of disasters on human communities have often shown that stable and well-functioning groups can
be destroyed by events which are beyond their control. Moreover,
it is not unusual for the breakdown of a traditional community to
result in an overall demoralization and depression among individuals who no longer have the social support upon which they have
traditionally depended (see, e.g., Erikson's [1976] description of
how a natural disaster [a flood] caused a tremendous amount of
social disorganization in what had been a well-integrated and
functioning rural community). Yet, it is clear that despite the
negative effects we have described, by and large Japanese Americans remained remarkably psychologically healthy and the ethnic
community, although changed in many ways, was intact throughout the whole ordeal. Indeed, at the end of the war, the Japanese
American community was in some ways stronger than it had been
before December 7, 1941.

The critical question, then, is why were Japanese Americans able
to survive as well as they did? Certainly, one contributing factor
was their culture which emphasizes "bearing up" (*gaman*) and
perseverance at the individual level. In our view, however, what
was most directly responsible is that Japanese Americans were able
to maintain a meaningful community throughout the disruption.
For most, the community, although physically displaced, continued to act as a social context in which one was understood and
which provided a continuity with one's previous relationships.
Individuals were, of course, severely stressed by events out of their
control but they continued to have access to their long-standing
friendships and family relationships. Moreover, they recreated

many of the institutions which supported these relationships and with which they were familiar before incarceration. For example, they competed, as they had before the war, in a variety of well-organized and well-attended athletic leagues and celebrated all of the traditional Buddhist festivals. Being able to continue to find embeddedness in a collectivity which was experiencing the same events was thus a critical element in the survival of Japanese Americans both as individuals and as a community.

Further, their culture, which stresses the primacy of group survival over and above the retention of specific beliefs and practices, played an important role in the transition from a patriarchal Issei-dominated prewar community to a more egalitarian and assimilated postwar ethnic community. Although the Nisei were abruptly forced into leadership positions by the circumstances surrounding the evacuation and incarceration, they continued to provide energetic stewardship of the community in the postwar years.

REDRESS

The reparations movement, as it was initially called, or redress movement, as it was termed later, had its beginnings on the West Coast in the late 1960s when some Japanese Americans began calling for restitution for their imprisonment during World War II. In 1970, the JACL passed the first of three resolutions calling for reparations. By 1974, it was designated the priority issue for the organization. At the 1978 convention in Salt Lake City some parallels were drawn, and some significant differences noted, with respect to the experience of German Jews during World War II and the postwar restitution by the German government. At the conclusion of the meeting, the National Council unanimously passed a resolution specifying that $25,000 be allocated to each internee or his/her heir.

Unbeknownst to JACL leadership, Senator S. I. Hayakawa, the most prominent Japanese American opponent of redress, who had been invited to address the convention, made a comment to the media in which he characterized the incarceration as "good for the Nisei." Needless to say, this remark infuriated many members of the Japanese community, especially in light of the fact that during the war Hayakawa was a Canadian citizen who was living in Chicago and thus was not interned himself.

Nevertheless, the controversy surrounding Hayakawa's remarks reflects the fact that the Japanese American community has not always been united in its support for redress. When the issue was first discussed, many were fearful that there would be a backlash and that their much greater recent acceptance by the larger society would be jeopardized. The following are the thoughts of two Sansei on why some of the Nisei were reluctant to get involved in the redress issue:

> You'll find most Nisei are very reluctant to talk about redress . . . especially in Hood River. Because they're still living within that community. Their feeling is, "You know, you people in Portland, you say all you want about redress and stir waters. But, we have to live here and we have to get along with our neighbors, and so . . . we can't really say how we feel." [Ng 1989, 16]

Another Sansei realizes that her parents' responses are based upon the previous strained relationship with the white community and the tenuous, friendly coexistence that the Nisei have worked hard to establish:

> I think politically, it's a sensitive issue for the Japanese community in Hood River. Because they remember how difficult it was when the relationship was strained and [they] worked hard to develop a positive relationship with their Caucasian community. So having this issue raised . . . I'm sure will raise some sensitivities about that because it means that the problems that they faced in the past was from these relationships [with the Caucasians] of that related to the camps, and that's very sensitive for them. [Ng 1989, 16]

Others thought that although the cause was just, politically it simply was an impossible task. A minority felt that any monetary compensation would demean and trivialize their experiences. With the movement's slow but steady success, however, it came to be supported by virtually the entire Japanese American community.

The advice of the Japanese American congressional delegation was to first bring the circumstances surrounding the incarceration to the attention of the media and the public by pushing for the formation of a congressional fact finding commission. This was viewed by some in the ethnic community as a weak move that would only waste time. Nonetheless, the Commission on the Wartime Relocation and Internment of Civilians (CWRIC) came into being in 1980. Its prestigious members included Joan Z. Bernstein, Hon. Arthur J. Goldberg, Dr. Arthur S. Fleming, Hon. Hugh B. Mitchell, Hon. Edward W. Brooke, Hon. William M. Marutani, Hon. Daniel E. Lungren, Father Robert Drinan, and Father Ishmael V. Gromoff.

After holding hearings in several major cities and taking the testimony of over 750 persons, the Commission published its findings in *Personal Justice Denied* (Commission on Wartime Relocation and Internment of Civilians 1982). Its conclusion was that the incarceration was the product of "race prejudice, war hysteria and a failure of political leadership." Its recommendations included compensating each living victim $20,000. After concerted lobbying efforts by the Japanese American community, pushing from Japanese American legislators, and support from groups such as the Jewish lobby, the Civil Liberties Act of 1988 was signed into law by President Reagan. It mandates that the government make a formal apology for its actions toward Japanese Americans during World War II and a token payment of $20,000 to all living internees. The total appropriation will amount to $1.2 billion.

Only in the 1980s with the discussion and soul searching associated with the successful redress movement has the community as a whole cleansed itself of many of the repressed and unresolved feelings toward the incarceration. Prior to this time, many individuals felt pressure to present the incarceration and Japanese Americans' reaction to it in a way which would not "put off" the white community. With the greater acceptance of Japanese Americans by the larger society, with the United States becoming more racially tolerant and multicultural in its outlook, and with strong feelings within the community being dissipated by time, the political and psychological need for a nonthreatening interpretation of events has lessened considerably. Thus, for example, a wide range of individual and family reactions to the internment are now viewed by Japanese Americans as legitimate. Most Japanese Americans today see volunteering for the 442nd Regimental Combat Team or resisting the draft at Heart Mountain as honorable and understandable responses to an extremely difficult situation.

FOUR

POSTWAR ASSIMILATION

 Sociologists have long observed that the children of immigrants characteristically make a concerted effort to fit into the culture and lifestyle of the country to which their parents have immigrated. This type of immersion is referred to as "cultural assimilation" or "acculturation" in order to distinguish it from the generally more difficult obstacle for immigrant groups, which is actually to interact on an equal basis with other Americans in schools, in the workplace, in the neighborhood, and finally in dating and marriage. The latter process is referred to as "structural assimilation" (Gordon 1964, 71). This is not to say, of course, that structural assimilation is necessarily desirable. There are often quite serious costs associated with moving into the mainstream of American society (Novak 1972).

Every group of people who have come to the United States has a unique history with respect to structural assimilation and certainly some groups have had to deal with more difficult obstacles than others in this regard. At one extreme are Americans of African descent, who have experienced a type of forced exclusion, first in slavery and then in segregation, which no other group has had to endure for such a long period of time. At the other extreme are many groups from culturally similar northwest Europe who were accepted fairly rapidly by the majority group, so long as they learned English and showed proper loyalty to their adopted nation. Most of the immigrants from Southern and Eastern Europe fall somewhere in the middle of this continuum, insofar as they were never excluded continuously, as were blacks, or periodically, as were Japanese Americans, but nonetheless did experience discrimination and certainly were not accepted by majority group Americans in the workplace, the neighborhood, and especially in the home for some time after their ancestors reached the United States (see, e.g., Novak 1972).

What makes the case of Japanese Americans unique is the speed of their structural assimilation following World War II, given the degree to which they were discriminated against during the prewar and wartime periods. As we described earlier, from the very early days of their entry into the United States, the Japanese were viewed with great suspicion, not only by the majority group, but also by non-Anglo Saxon immigrants and their descendants. It will be recalled, for example, that most of the labor unions specifically excluded Japanese and other Asians from their ranks (see chapter 1). During the hysteria leading up to the evacuation and incarceration, very few individuals or groups came to the defense of Japanese Americans. Old stereotypes about the inability of the Japanese to "fit in" to mainstream America were rekindled with a vengeance (see chapter 2). It was surprising, then, that soon after being released from the camps Japanese Americans moved rapidly into educational and occupational areas from which they were traditionally excluded. Finally, and most dramatic of all, marriages between Japanese Americans and whites increased very rapidly after the war. Indeed, less than four decades after the incarceration half of all new marriages involving Japanese Americans were with whites (Kitano et al. 1984).

The question that naturally arises, then, is why was there such a rapid turn of events with respect to the assimilation of Japanese Americans? The answer is quite complex, but it involves an interaction between changes in the structure of American society during the immediate postwar years, purposive actions by government authorities, a pent-up set of resources which Japanese Americans had built up during the prewar period, and cultural characteristics of Japanese American community life.

The postwar economic boom meant that Japanese Americans were able to operate in an environment in which there was a great demand for their skills and, most important, much less competition between them and white Americans for desirable jobs. The American economy as a whole was expanding and Japanese Americans, along with other Americans, were able to take advantage of these new opportunities. At the same time, government policies and actions, especially those of the WRA, led to their geographical dispersion which, in turn, discouraged the recreation of ethnic enclaves.

The role played by Japanese American culture in the rapid postwar movement toward structural assimilation was multifaceted. Perhaps best known is the way in which the values fostered by the Japanese American family and community and reinforced through participation in the ethnic small business economy produced a huge amount of human capital in the form of high levels of education and a strong "work ethic" that could be utilized as soon as discriminatory barriers were loosened (Fujimoto 1975; Nee and Wong 1985).

Equally important, however, is the fact that Japanese American culture contains some core elements which make it possible for people to adapt to different circumstances with less difficulty than would be the case if they were operating from another cultural basis. In particular, the principle that group survival is more important than specific aspects of traditional culture meant that they did not struggle as much as they might have with the normal process of giving up some of the "old ways" of the immigrant culture in order to fit in with the majority group. The key point here is that it was less costly for Japanese Americans to give up aspects of traditional culture which other groups have found to be quite traumatic simply because in the Japanese way of looking at the world such compromises are permissible so long as they promote group survival and prosperity.

Nevertheless, just as there were differences between the experiences of Japanese Americans in Hawaii and the mainland during the prewar and wartime years, so too were there substantial differences in their respective struggles with structural assimilation in the postwar era. Although the immigrant Issei started out in both locations as low-paid, exploited laborers, opportunities for participation in higher status jobs opened up more rapidly for Hawaiian than for West Coast Japanese prior to World War II. This is seen especially in public sector employment, where, for example, substantial numbers of certified Japanese teachers were hired in the

Hawaiian public school systems but only a handful were as fortunate in California (Kitano 1976, 97–98, 173–176).

THE HAWAIIAN CASE

In a number of important ways, the postwar Hawaiian economy did not provide the opportunities available on the West Coast, largely due to the narrow base of the Islands' economic structure, which depended mainly on tourism, military bases, and plantations. Nevertheless, the Hawaiian Japanese still had a tremendous advantage over their West Coast counterparts in not having experienced the economic and psychic costs of internment. Perhaps even more important, although the infrastructure of the West Coast ethnic communities was severely disrupted by the concentration camp experience, the infrastructure of the Hawaiian Japanese community remained largely intact, giving it a political advantage as well.

One of the catalysts for translating the potential power of the Hawaiian Japanese community into a viable political force was the return of the 442nd soldiers. The travels, much-publicized decorations, and opportunities to interact with a wide variety of people and institutions dramatically raised the expectations and self-confidence of these young men. Residents noticed, as one Japanese American schoolteacher put it, that they had a "belligerent, chip-on-the-shoulder, I've fought-the-war-now-I-demand-full-rights" attitude (Kotani 1985, 132–133). In short, they were not willing to settle for second class citizenship. A number of these veterans went to law school with the aid of the GI Bill. They also formed the 442nd Veterans Club, which helped them to mobilize their collective resources.

Before World War II, the Japanese in Hawaii had an increasing although still relatively weak role in Hawaiian government. This is clearly reflected in the number of elected and appointed officials of Japanese ancestry in Hawaiian government in the prewar period. The number remained relatively small until 1940 when it jumped sharply. Yet, even after this increase the number of Japanese appointed officials remained low. By 1950, however, that number had increased to more than three times what it had been before the war (see appendix 10 for more details).

In large part, these changes can be attributed to simple demographics. In 1930, only 12 percent of the eligible voters in the territory were of Japanese ancestry. By 1950, the figure had reached 40 percent. With the passage of the McCarran-Walter Act in 1952, the Issei finally were given the right to citizenship; this further increased the political clout of the Japanese.

In addition, World War II weakened the power of sugar plantation owners, up to that point the dominant elite. Martial law, which was enacted throughout the Islands, transferred power from this economic elite to a military bureaucracy. Moreover, the war changed Honolulu into a modern city with wide job opportunities, especially in the burgeoning tourist industry, thus reducing the economic leverage of the plantation owners over workers. During this period, managerial positions began to open up for minorities as the old paternalistic officers were replaced by more profit-driven corporate leaders from the mainland (Ogawa 1978, 353–356).

Before World War II, the dominant Republican party was supported and controlled by the sugar plantation interests. A rehabilitated Democratic party thus became the vehicle for the postwar Nisei effort to pursue ethnic interests in politics. A central figure in this process was John Burns, a Honolulu police captain who during the war defended the Nisei when their loyalty was impugned. In 1948, Burns formed an alliance with then–University of Hawaii undergraduate Daniel Inouye, who convinced the 442nd Veterans Club that they could help improve the social and political status of the Japanese by becoming actively involved in the Democratic party (Ogawa 1978, 381). By 1954, Burns and his Democratic coalition won almost two-thirds of the state Senate and more than two-thirds of the House. Almost half of these legislators were Nisei, most of the new members being war veterans and recent law school graduates (Kotani 1985, 136).

Given the successful postwar push of Hawaii's Japanese into politics, it was clearly in their interest for the territory to gain statehood, the ultimate affirmation of their desire to achieve first class citizenship. In fact, the Japanese were among the strongest supporters of statehood. A survey taken in 1958, for example, showed that 62 percent of the Japanese favored statehood, compared to 44 percent of the Chinese, 33 percent of the whites, and 30 percent of the native or part native Hawaiians (Fuchs 1961, 412).

Attempts to develop statehood legislation in Congress had begun as early as 1930, but they had been blocked, in part by racist sentiments, especially among Southern Congressmen. In 1947, for example, a representative from Georgia argued:

> What does it [the Hawaii bill] do? It makes citizens with rights with you and me of 180,000 Japanese. . . . It gives these people the same rights you and I have; we the descendants of those who created, fought and maintained this country. . . . When you give these people the same rights we have today, you will have two Senators speaking for those 180,000 Japanese. [Ogawa 1978, 384–385]

With an increase in pressure from statehood proponents in Hawaii as well as the emergence of the civil rights movement on the mainland, however, the statehood movement began to gain more supporters in Congress. Finally, on March 12, 1959, the 85th Congress voted to make Hawaii the fiftieth state in the Union. This was an important tribute to the development of Hawaii's institutions and its polyglot mixture of peoples. For the Japanese, it marked the end of a long struggle for first class status and completed what Ogawa (1978) has characterized as "the bloodless revolution."

THE PACIFIC COAST

Prior to the incarceration, there were some isolated attempts to create segregated schools in San Francisco and the Sacramento Delta region, but by and large Japanese Americans were never totally segregated from white society in the way that blacks were excluded. The vast majority of Nisei, except those who were sent back to Japan to be educated (these persons are called Kibei), attended public elementary and high schools with Caucasian children. Nevertheless, most of their social contacts outside of the classroom and the athletic field were restricted to fellow Japanese.

During the thirties, when the first of the Nisei generation were coming of age, a significant number were able to obtain a higher education in West Coast universities, sometimes at great personal and familial cost. Yet most were blocked from using their newly acquired skills because of the discrimination they faced in mainstream business, the professions, and government. Often they were forced to return to the ethnic economy with its low prestige and hard physical labor as well as subjection to the authority of their parents or parents' friends who typically ran the farm or the fruit stand (Bonacich and Modell 1980, 84–92). Thus, the prewar Japanese community contained considerable human capital resources that were held in check by discrimination.

A few scholars (e.g., Modell 1977, 135) have argued that by the 1930s the Issei wanted to maintain the "color line" in agriculture so as to preserve their economic niche. A more plausible view, however, is that like most American parents the Issei would have preferred that their children "advance" to more prestigious and lucrative jobs, especially given their educational achievements. In any event, this issue soon became moot as the Issei-dominated ethnic economy was destroyed during the war. When the Nisei left the relocation centers they commonly started on the bottom rungs of the organizational and occupational ladders, but the elimination of tension with Japan, the heroism of the 442nd Regimental Combat Team, and the rapidly expanding postwar economy combined to generate a much more open opportunity structure for them than had ever been experienced by Japanese Americans before the war. This was especially true in the Midwest and East. Because of their educational achievements, the pent-up human capital of the community was quickly translated into movement into middle class American society, in spite of some remaining vestiges of discrimination in housing and employment.

Some writers, both Japanese Americans and others from outside the ethnic community, have proposed what might be termed the "minority success story." This view explains the speed of Japanese American occupational and residential assimilation principally in terms of their quiet perseverance and hard work (e.g., Hosokowa 1969; Peterson 1970). By implication, this view would seem to argue that, for whatever reasons, most other minority groups have not been as successful as the Japanese because they have not worked as hard and have not been as persistent in their efforts to "quietly" overcome discrimination.

Many third and fourth generation Japanese Americans find this "model minority" image offensive, as do persons in other minority groups to whom the Japanese have been compared (see Gee 1976;

Tachiki et al. 1971). In their view, it paints an oversimplified picture of Japanese American and, more generally, Asian American success. Since this group is "successful" no resources need to be allocated to deal with its unique problems. Moreover, if one accepts the model minority logic then presumably any group can be successful in America through perseverance and hard work. Even if one ignores the political implications of the model minority perspective, it is a gross oversimplification of what transpired in Japanese American communities after World War II. A more accurate interpretation must recognize the resource base of Japanese Americans on the eve of World War II, the role of particular historical events and government policies, and the specific characteristics of Japanese culture and social organization.

ETHNIC RESOURCES, CULTURE, AND GOVERNMENT ACTIONS

The situation of Japanese Americans during the 1930s can best be described as that of a group which had considerably more resources, in terms of education, family and ethnic group solidarity, and economic experience (largely through the ethnic economy) than many American ethnic groups at corresponding points in their respective ethnic group life cycles. Although a substantial portion of the Japanese population was engaged in menial positions in labor intensive enterprises, especially in agriculture, their educational achievements were actually higher than those of white Americans. In 1940, for example, 23.1 percent of Japanese adults in the U.S. were high school graduates and 5.0 percent were college graduates, compared to corresponding figures of 15.1 percent and 4.9 percent for Caucasian Americans (see appendix 9 for comparative figures on numbers of persons in different groups having completed four or more years of college).

The events of World War II cost Japanese Americans very dearly in terms of economic and psychological damage, leaving a legacy which is still visible. However, some of these events set the stage for the accelerated movement of the second generation Nisei into the mainstream of American life. Almost immediately, the defeat of Japan removed the tainted association of Japanese Americans with a powerful, non-Western adversary. At the same time, the emergence of the cold war meant that Japan became a vital element in furthering American interests in the Far East.

Moreover, the United States experienced a very strong postwar economic boom, creating occupational opportunities that, unlike those available in the Depression era in the 1930s, did not threaten dominant group interests. Relocated Nisei quickly established a reputation for being good workers and were sometimes even recruited by employers on the streets in cities with labor shortages (Albert 1980, 116).

In addition, the WRA actively encouraged the Japanese to disperse geographically to minimize hostility. The authorities felt that the recreation of the West Coast Nihonmachis or Japantowns would retard the ethnic group's reentry into the mainstream. They even discouraged the Japanese from being seen together in groups. In part, this dispersion was a product of the fact that before January 1945 the Japanese could not return to their homes in the Western Defense Zone. They were forced to relocate in the Midwest or East if they wanted to leave the internment camps. However, even after the West Coast was reopened, approximately one-third of the resettlers chose to relocate to the East and Midwest. This was due in part to the some thirty documented acts of terrorism against the early resettlers, principally in the farming communities of central California (Girdner and Loftis 1969). Further, there was some resentment among the internees about returning to communities from which they had been "kicked out."

The issue of whether to recreate ethnic neighborhoods and institutions was one of the most hotly debated topics in the Japanese American community at that time. The Issei, not surprisingly, were in favor of rebuilding many of the ethnic institutions they had controlled before the war. Not only did the majority still have a language problem, but they also wanted to reestablish authority over their Nisei children who had escaped much of their influence during the disruptive days of evacuation, incarceration, and relocation. Many Nisei, on the other hand, did not want to return to what they saw as the constraining prewar community and thought that the Japanese should take this opportunity to assimilate into the institutions of the larger society.

One of the more common areas where this intergenerational

conflict surfaced was on the question of whether to create new churches with ethnically segregated congregations or to join predominantly Caucasian churches in their neighborhoods. Another source of conflict was the question of whether language schools should be reinstituted. Some Nisei viewed their reestablishment as anachronistic.

The incarceration and the WRA policy of dispersal also had an important effect on the subsequent demographic profile of the Japanese population by accelerating the process of urbanization. As noted earlier, even in the 1920s and 1930s the Japanese American population was much more heavily involved in agriculture than Americans as a whole. At the beginning of World War II, almost 50 percent of the members of this group were employed in some phase of agriculture. Undoubtedly many prewar Japanese farming families would have followed the national pattern of moving from the farm to the city and suburban areas after the war, but the forced evacuation of these families from productive lands clearly pushed more people off the land than would have left on their own. Because most left the relocation centers with little in the way of assets, they often virtually had no choice but to take wage earning positions in the expanding metropolitan areas.

The acceptance of Japanese Americans was enhanced considerably by the highly publicized record of the Nisei 442nd Regimental Combat Team and the 100th Infantry Battalion. Their actions demonstrated to the American public "in blood" where the loyalties of the Nisei really lie. Both the Hawaiian volunteers and the smaller number of internees who came straight out of the mainland camps realized that their actions would have a strong impact on the acceptance of the Japanese after the war. This overarching purpose no doubt provided much of the motivation for the unit to become the most decorated of its size in American military history. Further, the Army, the WRA, and often the press, particularly in Hawaii, used their record to fight anti-Japanese prejudice.

A critical element in the prewar Japanese American experience in terms of their postwar assimilation was their disproportionate involvement in small-scale business enterprises. Although in many instances they suffered a total loss of their economic assets during internment, it is clear that the values learned while living in a small business family became an important form of "human capital"

which subsequent generations used in professional and managerial pursuits once such opportunities presented themselves
(Fujimoto 1975; O'Brien and Fugita 1982). Fujimoto refers to this as
an "entrepreneurial ideology" which

> no doubt stemmed from the Issei's experiences which modified and
> shaped their lives in America in major ways. The Issei as entrepre-
> neurs transmitted these values and ideologies to the Nisei children.
> As a matter of fact, the Nisei children were expected to assume their
> share of the work as soon as they were old enough, particularly when
> the family was engaged in farming or in running a small shop or hotel.
> [Fujimoto 1975, 88]

The transmission of the entrepreneurial ideology means that
while later generations may struggle with earlier ones over some
traditional behaviors, such as language use, there remains a fundamental continuity in the constellation of core values pertaining
to the small scale entrepreneur's work ethic. These values are not
only consistent with but reinforce the collectivistic community
concepts which were crucial in establishing the economic and
social accommodation of the first generation.

The ability of the second generation Nisei to move into the
mainstream of American life without cutting off their roots from
the larger Japanese American experience and community also was
facilitated by the "relativistic" ethic inherent in Japanese culture.
As noted earlier, Japanese culture sees cultural content like language or even religion as clearly secondary to the preservation of
the group itself (Reischauer 1981, 138–145). This has meant that at
critical points in Japanese history, there has been an incorporation
of foreign cultural elements, first Chinese and later Western, when
it facilitated group survival. Similarly, Japanese Americans have
been able to adopt many mainstream American values, lifestyles,
and other characteristics which have facilitated their assimilation
into the larger society without having to relinquish many of their
ties to the Japanese American community.

This pattern departs markedly from the one experienced by
many European ethnic communities where frequently an intense
struggle occurred between the forces of assimilation, which
sought, by and large, to have the immigrants give up many of their
traditional values and perspectives, and the old guard in the ethnic

community, which sought to retain these cultural items (see, e.g., Hofstader 1955a; Whyte 1981). For the Japanese, however, issues like language or even religion are not terribly problematic since the real core of the ethnic experience and culture is the preservation of the social group (see Reischauer 1981, 138–145).

POSTWAR EDUCATIONAL CHARACTERISTICS

Because of the Meiji-era Japanese government's policy of universal education, the Issei immigrants arrived in the U.S. and Hawaii with a level of education that was quite high compared to that of many other immigrant groups. Moreover, their involvement in small business supported values like hard work and initiative, which encouraged educational achievement. Thus, even in 1940, the percentage of college graduates among the Japanese was actually slightly higher than that of white Americans (5.0% compared to 4.9%). In subsequent years, the proportion of college graduates increased significantly more rapidly among Japanese Americans than among white Americans. By 1970, 15.9 percent of persons of Japanese ancestry were college graduates, whereas only 11.3 percent of white Americans had achieved that educational level. By 1980, the gap had widened even further, with 26.4 percent of the former and 17.4 percent of the latter having completed four years of college (see appendix 9 for more details).

It is interesting to note, however, that the rate of increase in completing four years of college still is much greater among Chinese Americans than among Japanese Americans. In 1940, for example, the Chinese had a smaller number of college graduates (3.0%) than did the Japanese but their percentages rose much more rapidly, so that by 1970 there were almost 10 percent more college graduates among the Chinese than among the Japanese (25.6% compared to 15.9%; see appendix 9).

In part, the greater educational achievements of the Chinese vis-à-vis the Japanese are due to the fact that substantial numbers of Chinese professionals came to the United States during and immediately after World War II when the Communists took power on the mainland. Further, because of the occupational preferences established in the 1965 Immigration Reform Act, there has been a large secondary migration of highly educated persons from Taiwan.

94

POSTWAR OCCUPATIONAL CHARACTERISTICS

The opening up of employment opportunities for Japanese Americans following their release from the camps is one of the most dramatic changes in the history of this ethnic group. This is most evident in the increase in their numbers in professional services and public administration, occupations from which they had been virtually excluded on the mainland prior to 1945. In 1930, for example, there were only forty-one persons of Japanese extraction in public administration, accounting for a mere one-tenth of one percent of the Japanese labor force at that time. By 1960, however, that figure had jumped to 6.6 percent. What is even more impressive, by 1980 over one-fifth (21.8%) of employed persons in the Japanese American community were involved in professional services. The largest area of employment, however, remains that of trade (both retail and wholesale), finance, insurance, and real estate, constituting 35.9 percent of employment by persons of Japanese ancestry (see appendix 5).

As noted earlier, there was also a substantial drop in the numbers of Japanese involved in the traditional occupational niche of agriculture. The percentage fell from 45.2 in 1930 to 14.2 in 1960, 7.4 in 1970, and 4.8 in 1980. It should be noted here that the last figure is still higher than that of the general population (only 3.0% were involved in agriculture in 1980; see appendix 7).

Although they no longer have an "ethnic hegemony" over truck crops (Jiobu 1988), the ability of Japanese Americans to organize collectively has given them considerable influence in the agricultural economy of California. This was illustrated a few years ago by the impact of the Nisei Farmers League in a farm-labor dispute. This San Joaquin Valley growers' organization, which was started by small and middle-size Japanese American farmers, was successful in organizing significant numbers of white as well as Japanese American growers and eventually played a major role in state agricultural politics (Fugita and O'Brien 1977; O'Brien and Fugita 1984).

Moreover, there is evidence to show that in an area like Los Angeles, where there are large concentrations of Japanese Americans, there remains a substantial amount of community involvement in ethnic enterprises. For example, there is a tendency for

Japanese Americans in these areas to patronize the grocery stores, restaurants, real estate offices, and professional services of fellow ethnics (Fugita and O'Brien 1991).

A number of researchers have suggested that the impressive gains registered by Japanese Americans following World War II may mask some remaining discrimination against them in the workplace. In particular, they have raised the question of whether Japanese Americans, or for that matter Asians in general, receive as much of a return on their educational investment as do white Americans. In their view, the income gap between whites and Asians of comparable educational levels is evidence of the persistence of discrimination (e.g., Cabezas and Kawaguchi 1988; Woodrum 1981).

An alternative thesis is that Japanese and other Asian Americans do not fully realize their occupational potential in corporate settings because their ethnic culture does not maximize the return on educational investment—discouraging, for example, individualistic assertiveness (Hraba 1979, 332; Iwata 1988). It may be that Japanese American interpersonal style, which still places primary emphasis on promoting group harmony and deflecting attention from oneself, is less effective in gaining recognition in the more individualistic setting of American corporate life. In support of this view is the finding that Japanese Americans who live apart from the concentrated ethnic population on the West Coast occupy more professional positions overall (Levine and Rhodes 1981, 47), which suggests that moving away from the ethnic community may lessen the influence of traditional Japanese values pertaining to modesty and reserve and, conversely, may encourage Japanese Americans to develop more of the American core culture's individualistic assertiveness. An equally plausible explanation is that those individuals who have more human capital resources and motivation to begin with are more likely to relocate to areas outside of their traditional home on the West Coast.

Certainly, as we will see in the next chapter, there is considerable evidence of the persistence of distinctive personality traits and an interactional style in the Japanese American population and that these characteristics can be traced back to traditional Meiji-era Japanese values and outlooks. Indeed, Harry Kitano, among others, has suggested that because of their isolation from the events which were constantly modifying the culture of Japan, contemporary Japanese Americans, like contemporary French Canadians, may more clearly reflect the traditional nineteenth century culture of Japan than do the contemporary citizens of that nation (1976, 118–119). If this thesis is even partially true then it at least complicates the issue of determining the sources of the remaining, and more subtle, discrimination against Japanese Americans. On a more general level, it may be but a special case of the larger issue of how Japanese Americans relate to the core culture, lifestyles, and social organization of contemporary mainstream America. This is an important matter which we will discuss more fully in the remaining chapters.

CHANGING FAMILY FORMS AND INTERMARRIAGE

The decline of the ethnic-based agricultural and small shopkeeper economies following the evacuation and internment has had profound effects on the traditional structure of the Japanese American family. Not only was the patriarchal position of the Issei father weakened by these events, but it also moved many Japanese Americans from a family structure that was based on an economic production unit to the more typical American arrangement of independent nuclear families whose economic base rested on wages or salaries earned outside of the family.

In the wage earning situation, the family is no longer the unit of both production and consumption. Moreover, the oldest son no longer has a family firm to inherit. As a result, there is no "official inheritance" of the Japanese household, which was an important source of continuity and solidarity in the prewar ethnic communities. Postwar inheritance typically has been consistent with mainstream American norms which emphasize equality in the distribution of material resources among the children. Thus the household has lost much of its economic and symbolic significance (Yanagisako 1985).

This change to a more individualistic inheritance pattern has created some confusion and conflict. There have been instances, for example, when Nisei assumed that inheritance would follow the mainstream American pattern but became resentful when an Issei parent who was following the traditional inheritance model did not divide all of his/her property equally. Alternatively, if the Issei parent followed the typical American inheritance pattern and divided the property equally or provided something extra for the child who took care of him/her or the most needy member of the family, then a Nisei eldest son was disappointed that he did not receive control of the family material resources. The son saw the undivided inheritance as the equivalent of the traditional family firm and as the appropriate Japanese inheritance pattern (Yanagasako 1975).

By far the greatest change in the family life of Japanese Americans since the end of World War II has been the increase in the amount of intermarriage with Caucasians. Numerous students of immigration and minority group relations have pointed out that intermarriage is the most sensitive indicator of the relationship between two groups (Gordon 1964). Almost as soon as the Japanese began immigrating in significant numbers until after World War II legal and social sanctions existed on the West Coast against their intermarrying with Caucasians. Antimiscegenation laws were in force in California, for example, from 1905 until 1948. The following statement by a white minister in California in 1913 illustrates the intensity of majority group feeling on this issue in the early years of Japanese immigration:

> Near my home is an eighty-acre tract of as fine land as there is in California. On that tract lives a Japanese. With that Japanese lives a white woman. In that woman's arms is a baby. What is that baby? It isn't white. It isn't Japanese. It is a germ of the mightiest problem that ever faced this state; a problem that will make the black problem of the South look white. [Spickard 1980]

Not surprisingly, the intermarriage rate for Issei men in California was a mere 2 percent. The Nisei, who came of age about the time of the incarceration were not as socially isolated as their parents, since most of them had attended integrated public schools, but they too had an extremely low intermarriage rate, 4 percent, which compares with a rate of 20 percent among second generation European ethnics (Spickard 1980). By the 1970s, however, intermarriage among the third generation Sansei had jumped to approximately 60 percent of all new marriages (Kitano et al. 1984).

It should also be noted that the Japanese, like many other immigrant groups, had strong norms against outmarrying. Since marriage was inextricably tied to the preservation of the family's name and honor, a good deal of effort was placed in finding suitable partners through "go-betweens." Those from lower social backgrounds and those who came from families with poor health histories were to be avoided.

In fact, a large percentage of the Nisei marriages before the war were at least partially arranged. Most often this "legitimation" was accomplished through the use of a "go-between" and the help of the families involved. For example, a man might want to develop a relationship with a particular woman whom he had seen at a community function. His family would then arrange for the proper introductions to be made with the help of a "go-between." The notion of an arranged or even partially arranged marriage is, of course, inconsistent with the concept of "romantic love" which is at the core of the general American culture. Thus, unless specifically asked, most Nisei will not volunteer information about the "arranged" qualities of their marriages.

It was not entirely unheard of for an Issei parent to threaten disowning a Nisei son or daughter who wanted to marry a Caucasian. Among Nisei parents, however, a more common response is the following one described by a Sansei woman: "Well my dad says it's okay to have friends of another race but it would be nice if you had a Japanese boyfriend. . . . He would rather have my real good friends be all Japanese and my casual friends be whatever" (Spickard in preparation)."

The low intermarriage rate among the Issei and Nisei has held down the current overall level of intermarriage among Japanese Americans in spite of the relatively high rates of intermarriage among the Sansei in the 1960s and 1970s. To put the current rate of intermarriage in perspective it is useful to compare different groupings of Americans with respect to whether or not they claim multiple ancestry. Multiple ancestry, of course, means that they are products of intermarriage. Among Northern European groups the rate of multiple ancestry is close to three-fourths (e.g., 74.3% among the Irish and 76.0% among the Swiss). Among some Southern and Eastern European ethnic groups who immigrated to this country during the same time period the figure is less than half of this (e.g.,

35.8% among the Greeks and 47.8% among the Ukrainians). Among the Japanese the current figure for multiple ancestry (i.e., 1980 census) is 15.7 percent (see appendix 4).

Nonetheless, even though the figures on multiple ancestry illustrate that the mixing in of the Japanese with the general U.S. population has a long way to go before this group disappears as a distinct racial and ethnic entity, it is clear that the trend toward full assimilation is quite strong. It is especially dramatic given the earlier racial antipathy toward Japanese Americans. The critical question, however, is, to what extent has this change impacted on the character of the Japanese American community? This will be the subject of our next chapter.

FIVE

THE PERSISTENCE OF COMMUNITY

 Traditionally, sociologists have viewed the assimilation of an immigrant group into a new society as inevitably leading to the loss of involvement in and attachment to the ethnic community. This process, it is argued, begins with the adoption of the more visible cultural characteristics of the larger society, then proceeds to the stage where the group interacts with persons from the majority group, first in work situations, then in their neighborhoods, and finally in intermarriage (e.g., Gordon 1964). The key assumption here is that the "ways" of the immigrants and those of the host society are in varying degrees incompatible and that there are inevitable pressures to cast aside old ways in order to fit better into the host society.

During the 1960s and 1970s, however, a number of books were written which challenged the argument just described. These scholars contended that what appeared to be a melting pot, in the case of European immigrants, in fact had not materialized. They suggested that persons in these groups still maintained distinctive lifestyles and values and, especially in large urban areas, ethnic community institutions (e.g., Glazer and Moynihan 1970; Novak 1972). Some also argued that "ethnogenesis," the emergence of new forms of ethnicity which have a minimal relationship to national origins (e.g., Greeley 1974), was taking place.

More recently, scholars have adopted a more complex view that ethnic groups vary considerably in the extent to which their members retain identification with and involvement in their ethnic community once they become assimilated into the larger society (e.g., Reitz 1980; Yancey, Ericksen, and Leon 1985). The descendants of the most frequently studied ethnic groups, Americans with European origins, still retain a "psychic" or "symbolic" connection to their country of origin (e.g., Gans 1979). This attachment remains an important part of their self identity even after several generations of structural assimilation into mainstream American life (Alba and Chamlin 1983). But, at the same time, for the vast majority in most of these groups, ethnic involvement does not go beyond the "psychic" level. Studies show, for example, that less than five percent of third generation Italian and Irish Americans belong to ethnic community organizations (Goering 1971; Roche 1982).

Other ethnic groups, such as Jewish and Japanese Americans, however, have maintained involvement in ethnic community affairs to a much greater degree. In our survey of Japanese Americans in California, for example, we found that over 50 percent of the respondents belonged to some kind of Japanese American voluntary association, not including churches, a figure ten times greater than the level of involvement found in the studies of the European immigrant groups referred to above. The ethnic organizations Japanese Americans belonged to included golf and fishing clubs, bowling leagues, business and professional groups, neighborhood associations, and cultural groups, as well as ethnic interest groups such as the Japanese American Citizens League (JACL) (Fugita and O'Brien 1991).

Most striking is the fact that Japanese American involvement in ethnic voluntary associations is actually higher in areas with a lower density of fellow ethnics. This suggests that in places where they are found in small numbers Japanese Americans make a special effort to create organizations that encourage community involvement. As Oguri-Kendis (1979) has pointed out, this is precisely the way Japanese Americans maintain high levels of interaction with one another in suburbia where the majority of them now live. Thus, even though they generally live and work in a "white world," much of their meaningful interaction takes place within the ethnic community. Interestingly enough, it is also in these areas of low ethnic density that the involvement of persons in mainstream, non-Japanese American voluntary associations is highest as well (O'Brien and Fugita 1983b).

The critical question, of course, is why do Japanese Americans maintain a high level of ethnic community involvement despite the fact that they have by and large moved into the mainstream of the larger society? Again, as in the case of their earlier history, the explanation for their adaptations can be found in an interaction between "structural constraints" which have limited their options, or at least *perceived* options, and the unique features of Japanese culture which have inclined persons in this ethnic group toward certain kinds of responses to problems. Let us look first at discrimination, perceived by Japanese Americans to be a structural factor that encourages them to maintain the cohesiveness of their ethnic community.

THE PERSISTENCE OF DISCRIMINATION

The role of discrimination in maintaining the involvement of Japanese Americans in their ethnic community can be viewed as operating on several levels. The number of actual experiences with visible and demeaning kinds of discrimination differ considerably by generation. At this level, most Nisei have vivid memories of the evacuation and incarceration as well as being discriminated against in their youth when they attempted to use public facilities such as swimming pools and theaters. The Sansei, on the other hand, have grown up in the more benign postwar era and have not had nearly as many personal experiences with the more visible forms of discrimination.

At another level, however, the vast majority of Japanese Americans perceive the persistence of less dramatic but nonetheless real incidences of prejudice and discrimination and this makes them aware of their common interests. Examples of this sort of annoying behavior include being confronted by teenagers making a mocking imitation of an "oriental" language or being called "Jap" by someone in a moving car. Japanese Americans also are occasionally reminded of their minority status by naive comments from whites about "how well they speak English." All of these actions call their "Americanness" into question and raise the possibility that they will never be fully accepted.

The fear of discrimination has been influenced by the current economic competition between the United States and Japan. Recently, for example, Vincent Chin, a Chinese American, was mistaken for a Japanese and beaten to death by unemployed Detroit auto workers. An increasing number of incidents such as this as well as attacks on immigrant Vietnamese fishermen in the waters off the coast of Texas and the murder of Southeast Asian school children in Stockton, California, make Japanese Americans and other Asian Americans sensitive to their minority status and the possible need to defend themselves against acts of discrimination or even violence. As a result, a number of Asian American organizations have begun to monitor, publicize, and aid victims of so-called hate crimes and to push governmental agencies to do the same (e.g., Harrison 1986).

The extent to which Japanese Americans see discrimination persisting is perhaps best reflected in responses to specific questions about job and social discrimination. Although only a minority of Nisei (31.3%) and Sansei (12.8%) report personal experiences with a "considerable amount" or a "great deal" of discrimination in their adult lives (which for both groups has been largely during the post–World War II period), a majority, 54.9 percent of the Nisei and 54.8 percent of the Sansei, believe that job discrimination against Japanese Americans *as a group* still exists. An even higher proportion, 76.0 percent of the Nisei and 74.3 percent of the Sansei, believe that Japanese Americans "currently experience social discrimination" (O'Brien and Fugita 1983a).

There is a widespread feeling among Japanese Americans in corporate and government settings that it is difficult to become a full fledged member of the "old boy network" and to make it into upper management. As we saw earlier, several studies suggest that Japanese Americans cannot convert their educational attainment into income and high status jobs as well as whites with comparable backgrounds (e.g., Cabezas and Kawaguchi 1988; Woodrum 1981). On the other hand, white managers have argued that the small number of Japanese Americans and other Asian Americans in upper management is largely due to their lack of "aggressiveness" and the necessary "leadership" qualities (Schwartz 1987). In fact, on standard, mainstream-normed instruments Japanese Americans have lower assertiveness scores than European Americans (e.g., Connor 1974). Moreover, the Japanese style of leadership (*nihonteki*) emphasizes low key, indirect, consensus building.

Given the much greater emphasis on an individualistic style of leadership at upper management levels, it may be that part of the problem is an interpersonal style mismatch. In recent years, however, there has been a growing interest in American management circles in learning more about Japanese managerial styles, prompted, of course, by the widely publicized success of Japanese companies in international competition.

In short, the organizational discrimination issue is quite complex. It would appear that the reality may involve a combination of subtle forms of discrimination as well as some culturally based characteristics of interpersonal style possessed by members of the ethnic group. In any event, it is clear that the persistence of a distinctive interpersonal style plays a key role in the maintenance of Japanese American community life.

INTERPERSONAL STYLE AND COMMUNITY INVOLVEMENT

As noted earlier, Japanese culture places a great deal of emphasis on group harmony and the avoidance of conflict. This world view stresses the importance of meeting one's obligations to the group and not drawing attention to oneself (e.g., Connor 1976; Weisz et al. 1984; Yamamoto and Wagatsuma 1980; Zander 1983).

Group-centered values are also present in Western cultural traditions, and indeed are found in some of their highest ideals, such as in the Gospel message of love and community. But Western cultural traditions also contain very powerful individualistic elements. Historically, then, the values of individualism and community have been engaged in a dialectic within Western thought, with one or the other being ascendant at different times and places. Since the end of the medieval social order and the eventual dominance of the marketplace, however, individualism clearly has governed Western thought (see Bellah et al. 1985; Fromm 1941; Hsu, 1983; and Lasch 1979 for discussions of the role of individualism in Western societies and some of the problems associated with it).

Japanese culture, on the other hand, contains no such dialectic between individualistic and communal elements. To this day, with all of its adaptation of Western technology and fashion (in fact, leadership in many of these areas), Japanese society is dominated by group-centered values. In a recent book on the Japanese economic system, Dore observes:

> The trouble with the Japanese is that they have never really caught up with Adam Smith—in spite of the fact that a British publisher with a new scholarly book on Smith or Ricardo can expect to sell half the edition in Japan. They don't *believe* in the invisible hand. They believe—like Mao unleashing the Cultural Revolution and all other good Confucianists—that you cannot get a decent moral society, not even an efficient society, simply out of the mechanisms of the market powered by the motivational fuel of self-interest, however clever, or even divinely inspired, those mechanisms may be. The morality has got to come from the hearts, the wills and motives, of the individuals in it. [1986, 1]

To most Westerners, the extent to which Japanese culture demands that individual needs and interests should be submerged to meet collective goals would be totally unacceptable. For instance, Kidder (1987) points out that there is no direct equivalent for the word "fairness" as Westerners know it in the Japanese language. This is because concerns about individual rights, and thus injustice, are overshadowed by the value placed on group harmony. The latter gives priority to respect, honor, humility and politeness. If someone claims that s/he finds something "unfair" it presents the possibility of creating conflict, which in turn could be disruptive to group harmony. Thus, even the Japanese patent system is structured so as to avoid conflict and promote cooperation by encouraging cross-licensing as opposed to exclusive control (Melloan 1988).

A classic illustration of the lengths to which the Japanese expect individuals to go in order to preserve group cohesiveness is provided by Kidder:

> A French correspondent served as a guest speaker in Japan, substituting for a friend who had previously accepted the engagement. Before delivering the speech, he explained to the audience that the friend was

not present because he was attending the birth of his child. The audience laughed. After the speech, a member from the audience came up to the speaker to explain the laughter. He said the audience found it odd and incongruous that a man would miss a work obligation to attend the birth of his child. Had it been a Japanese man who was supposed to deliver the speech, he would have come even if his father or mother had just died. He would have said at the end, "I'm sorry if my performance was not up to your expectations, but you see, my father just died, so I hope you'll please excuse me now." [1987, 35]

One of the principal means of maintaining group harmony and consensus in Japanese society is by emphasizing conformity to demanding social roles. As Lebra (1972) states, "the Japanese individual is trained morally as well as psychologically to be sensitized to the place he occupies in a social setting, to perform faithfully whatever role is assigned to him, and to respond to the expectations and evaluations of others." Japanese interpersonal style stresses politeness and awareness of the feelings of others. Because of this, Japanese patterns of speech are much more indirect than those used by most Americans. They are designed to minimize the possibility of offending others or revealing some aspect of the self that would best remain hidden. From a Japanese point of view, American directness is often perceived as brusque, blunt, or aggressive. Americans see directness as the most rational means to achieving a goal. The Japanese are also, of course, interested in achieving goals, but for them interpersonal relationships take priority (Miyamoto 1986–87). As Americans who have attempted to do business with the Japanese overseas have discovered, it is useless to try to push too quickly to negotiations about the "bottom line" until the interpersonal issues have first been resolved.

There are, of course, important differences between the behaviors and norms of second and third generation Japanese Americans, on the one hand, and overseas Japanese nationals on the other. In order to assimilate into American society, Japanese Americans have had to adopt many American practices and to give up many traditional Japanese cultural items. There is, however, considerable evidence that Japanese Americans still retain many Japanese forms of interacting which set them apart from other Americans, even though they may appear to be full participants in all aspects of life in the larger society.

A Japanese American social psychologist, Frank Miyamoto (1986–87), suggests that differences between Nisei and mainstream interpersonal styles is a major reason why the former feel a need to interact with one another on a regular basis. In addition to differences in the nature and degree of social sensitivity, Miyamoto points out that a key difference in Japanese versus American interactional style is *spontaneity*. American culture places less emphasis than does Japanese culture on preserving group harmony. Thus, in the American cultural setting, the individual is less concerned with the reactions of others. Consistent with this, American culture stresses, indeed rewards, spontaneity of expression whereas Japanese culture emphasizes reserve and caution.

Japanese Americans, especially the older Nisei generation, having been brought up to display a great deal of interpersonal sensitivity, enter interpersonal situations, in Miyamoto's words, "with their brakes on" (1986–87). As a result, Japanese Americans operate with a different "gear ratio" than do most other Americans. This lack of "natural" spontaneity makes them less comfortable when interacting with non–Japanese Americans. Miyamoto (1986–87) suggests that the large amount of joking among Nisei is an attempt to match the spontaneity level of mainstream interaction without risking offending the other party, since joking is not to be taken seriously.

Speaking of the difficulties which the Nisei have faced in interacting in a Caucasian world, Miyamoto observes that

> Americans are more spontaneous than the Japanese because they are freer to express their feelings and emotions, are not as restrained by considerations of the feelings of others, and are less concerned about the attitudes of others toward their own person. They are also more spontaneous because their attention is more directed to the subjective self, to [their] own feelings and interests, and they are better prepared to respond independently. The Nisei, habituated to focusing on the other, had the wrong habits on which to build spontaneity. . . .
>
> Spontaneity in social interaction is not an altogether positive quality, for it necessarily lacks the values which inhere in deliberate behavior. However, if interaction is geared to a high tempo, a person lacking spontaneity would have difficulty participating and would feel discomfort and dissatisfaction. Furthermore, spontaneity tends to

give interest to a person, and its absence tends to make him appear dull and boring. [1986–7, 38]

In our survey in California what is perhaps most striking is that even among the most assimilated portion of the Japanese American community, the third generation Sansei, there is a strong feeling that there remain large differences between Japanese and Caucasian ways of interacting. Slightly more than half (50.9%) of the Sansei reported that differences between Japanese and Caucasian ways persist in business. Slightly less than half (46.3%) saw such differences in social situations while 74.4 percent and 65.8 percent reported differences in interpersonal styles in church and family respectively (O'Brien and Fugita 1983a).

A good example is the way decisions are reached in Japanese and American core culture organizations. In most American organizations, after all are ostensibly given the opportunity to air their views, a vote is called for to determine the majority view and the course of action to be followed. In Japanese American organizations, on the other hand, a vote is almost never called for, except in the largest and most formal organizations. What commonly happens is that after those who have recognized expertise on the topic and those who feel strongly about the issue have spoken, a consensus gradually emerges. Sensing such a consensus, the chairperson either will summarize the consensus position him or herself or ask for the opinion of a respected person. After the chairperson or opinion leader has spoken, the chairperson will ask if everyone agrees with that position. He or she will then scan the group. Group members almost always indicate their approval nonverbally. Most decisions are thus arrived at "unanimously." With this decision-making style, persons can avoid finding themselves in public disagreement with others, which is generally a more stressful experience for Japanese and Japanese Americans than it is for core culture Americans.

Although all contractual relationships involve some noncontractual elements, at least in terms of the cultural norms that make individuals feel obligated to fulfill their part of a bargain (Durkheim 1933), Japanese and Japanese Americans emphasize these elements to a much greater extent than is typically found in the Western marketplace. This is especially true with respect to the maintenance of long-term economic relationships. One of the reasons for the success of Japanese business enterprises is that a Japanese producer will shun a cheaper supplier in order to maintain a long-standing relationship with a supplier who temporarily may not be able to match the competitor's price but who, in the long run, will feel obligated to support his or her firm when the need arises. In that sense, the Japanese and Japanese Americans have long "social memories" (Dore 1986, 1–7; Light 1972).

In areas of the country where there are only small numbers of Japanese Americans, persons in this ethnic group are more likely to experience problems because of the differences between their interactional style and that of most other Americans. Gehrie (1976), who conducted extensive interviews with third generation Sansei in Chicago, for example, found that many of them experienced intense feelings of isolation, not only from the larger Caucasian community but from their ethnic community as well. In effect, they did not feel they fit well in either world. One of Gehrie's respondents described his feelings about relating to whites in the following way: "It's just an odd feeling being different and you knowing that you're different. . . . You know they're being very nice to you, but you know that you don't belong, and that it won't get very intimate, it won't get very heavy" (1976, 375).

Another of Gehrie's respondents had mixed feelings toward his ethnic community:

> Others [Japanese Americans] . . . are in the community, they go to their Japanese church . . . and they feel in. (Interviewer: And you feel torn?) Well yeah, I guess you could say that. No not really torn . . . isolated, an outsider coming in and trying to play because I'm Japanese too. [1976, 375]

Another feeling frequently expressed by Gehrie's respondents was that the motivation for achievement was seen as external to the self, coming from teachers, parents, or others. One of the Sansei put it this way:

> I think I play sort of a role . . . much like the role of a good student, good worker. . . . I regret it now because I think I missed out on an awful lot. Because I was constantly getting good grades, listening to

the teachers, obeying them, doing well . . . I missed out on an awful lot. . . . I missed out on more of the socializing with the kids, the fooling around and just relaxing . . . and at work too I just cannot get out of that. It's this role I get into where I have to be well-behaved, correct, obedient . . . without a mind of my own. [1976, 372]

Gehrie concludes that for the most part his respondents do not report experiencing "a group of peers who mirror and support the developing self." He goes on to suggest that the "expectable" solution, apparent acceptance and identification with white people, may come at a high psychological cost.

Similar themes have been voiced by Asian American college students on white campuses. Some representative comments were recorded by Osajima (1989) as illustrations of "hidden injuries of race":

all through my childhood, I wanted to be, you know, white, and I'd look in the mirror and try to see ways of looking at myself as more white, my nose looks like this, if it was a little pointier, or my eyes or my head was shaped differently or something like that . . . I think it really started when guy-girl relationships began and it was weird to see all my friends who were white have these girls that started liking them and stuff, and I was, it doesn't seem that anyone likes me, I wonder why that's so? Maybe if I was white that would solve my problems. [Osajima 1989]

A common reaction of the students was to try to distance themselves from the stereotypic image of Asians as "nerdy." The student quoted above went on to say:

all through my life I've tried to not be the stereotype . . . like my hair . . . I didn't want the stereotypical bowl-like haircut, or just the hair that was parted like this, and really puffy and weird. But hair was a big deal for a while and then glasses were a big deal. I still hate wearing glasses sometimes cause whenever I put glasses on I think boy I really look stereotypically oriental you know . . . when I was younger, I'd see people that . . . looked like they would fit the stereotype and I'd just . . . don't want to be like that you know, don't associate me like that because I don't want to be like that.[Osajima 1989]

It should be emphasized that many of the sentiments just described are shaped by the reaction of majority culture persons to Japanese and other Asian Americans. In areas of the country where Japanese and other Asian Americans are concentrated, such as Hawaii and Southern California, whites interact with them more on an everyday basis and thus do not perceive them as an unknown element. This appears to have a salutary effect on the self concept of Japanese Americans. Gehrie's (1976) and Osajima's (1989) findings suggest that the ability of Japanese Americans to be comfortable with their place in American society will depend to a large extent on the opportunities they have to continue interacting with fellow ethnics. In fact, Johnson (1976) reports that the Sansei in Hawaii experience their ethnic subculture as a very positive component of their self concept. Here, and in Southern California, the ethnic group is large enough to form a viable subculture such that the sense of being a minority is muted. All of this calls attention to the critical role which Japanese American voluntary associations play in the lives of ordinary members of this ethnic group.

VOLUNTARY ASSOCIATIONS AND THE PERSISTENCE OF COMMUNITY

Given the perception among Japanese Americans that discrimination against their group still exists, and, perhaps even more important, the persistence of the view that there are distinctive differences in interpersonal style between Japanese Americans and other Americans, it is not surprising that interest group politics continues to play a significant role in mobilizing the community and reminding persons of their common interests. This has been seen most recently in the mobilization of almost the entire Japanese American community behind the redress campaign (see chapter 3).

Moreover, the relatively high educational and income levels of the group make possible a very extensive and intricate communication system which is not dependent on their geographic concentration. Thus, in many ways the Japanese situation is similar to that of American Jews who are largely assimilated into gentile neighborhoods and organizations and yet retain a highly effective ethnic social network even in the suburbs (e.g., Benkin 1978; Gendrot and Turner 1983).

Again, it is important to recognize that this capacity of Japanese Americans to mobilize their ethnic community has been buttressed by the Japanese cultural emphasis on forming and adapting voluntary associations to help preserve the viability of the group. In turn, this cultural phenomenon has been reinforced by many successful historical experiences of the Japanese and Japanese Americans, both overseas and in this country, in using formal associations for achieving collective goals (see Norbeck 1972).

Traditionally, these associations have had a greater potential for *social coercion* than typically would be the case with American voluntary associations, especially with respect to the sense of obligation individuals feel toward fellow members, who are seen as "quasi-kin." At the same time, however, the same culture which creates this sense of obligation is remarkably flexible with respect to the specific kind of goals which the organization will pursue and/or the specific forms which it will take to reach those objectives. This, as we have argued, accounts for the remarkable amount of persistence of community among Japanese Americans despite the obvious radical changes in their specific cultural content and lifestyles over three generations (see chapter 1; Hsu 1971; 1975).

When they arrived in this country, the Issei were helped in dealing with a new and often hostile society by associations that had semiofficial ties to the Japanese government. These Japanese Associations handled record keeping and other matters relevant to immigration on both sides of the Pacific. In addition, they provided technical assistance to the immigrants on practical matters such as how to raise crops with which they were not familiar (Ichioka 1977a).

Later, the Japanese Associations formed farmers' cooperatives which gave the immigrants, and their descendants, significant advantages in purchasing seeds, fertilizer, and tools as well as providing marketing conduits for their crops. Japanese voluntary organizations have also served as more generalized community interest mechanisms when threats to the group were faced, such as when the various alien land laws were passed during the early part of this century. The JACL, the largest Japanese organization in the United States with over 27,000 members, has mounted numerous campaigns to pursue the civil rights of Japanese Americans, including successful efforts to remove the remaining discriminatory laws in the 1940s and 1950s as well as the recent redress campaign. The Nisei Farmers League emerged as a growers' group in a farm labor dispute in the Central Valley of California in the early 1970s and eventually developed into a powerful lobbying organization in California state politics (Fugita and O'Brien 1977; O'Brien and Fugita 1984).

In short, almost from the very beginning of their stay in the United States, the Japanese community has had a formal organizational base—a critical factor in the preservation of ethnic community life as individuals have moved from concentrated ethnic ghettos, sections of small towns, and farming enclaves to predominantly white suburbs. In short, formal organizations have been an important factor in the preservation of contemporary Japanese American community life in large measure because they have been able to adjust their original purposes to deal with changes in the nature of the ethnic group itself and the challenges it faced.

The tendency of voluntary associations in all communities to try to perpetuate themselves, has been termed by one writer "organizational momentum" (Reitz 1980, 216–218). This momentum would appear to have been enhanced in the case of Japanese Americans by two factors. First, the simple fact of having a large number of effective formal organizations in an ethnic group's history increases the likelihood that at least some viable organizational structures will continue to survive. In addition, as we have noted, Japanese American culture encourages organizations to adapt to the peculiar constraints and demands of their environments at any particular point in time, thus further increasing the odds of organizational survival.

An interesting and typical example of organizational survival in the Japanese American community is the evolution of mutual aid societies. These initially were created to meet the economic needs of poor immigrants. Most major cities in the United States, for example, have a Japanese American mutual aid society which originally provided money for a decent burial for indigent Issei bachelors without families. These organizations have survived in spite of the fact that most Japanese Americans today are middle class and have family and ethnic community support networks.

Many of these associations have adapted by becoming a source of ethnic community integration. This is done, for example, by coordinating Memorial Day ceremonies in which a number of ethnic community organizations participate.

Japanese Americans, like other immigrant ethnic groups, created organizations specifically designed to transmit traditional cultural content from the old country. Those organizations, however, have been not nearly as important in the long run as the special interest associations (e.g., ethnic athletic leagues) which are developed around American cultural content. Most Nisei were forced by their parents to attend Japanese language schools in which they were exposed to the Japanese language as well as *shusin* (Japanese moral education) (Lebra 1972) but, as is typical of the second generation, they were more concerned with learning American ways and often attended these schools with some degree of reluctance if not downright resentment. Nonetheless, these same persons subsequently created a wide variety of Nisei businessmen's associations, civic clubs, and recreational organizations which are found throughout the West Coast.

Such organizations have provided Japanese Americans with an environment in which they can interact comfortably with others who share a similar interpersonal style and yet, at the same time, be involved in an activity which is consistent with their American experience. Thus, these associations play a crucial role not only in the preservation of the ethnic community but also in support of the mental health of its individual members. They have served to combine critical aspects of ethnic community life with content from the mainstream of American life.

One of the reasons why these ethnic associations remain attractive and satisfying to Japanese Americans at the psychological level is that fellow ethnics have retained the group-centered value system. Fellow ethnics are seen as more socially predictable and responsible than other Americans. Thus, although Japanese Americans frequently admire and often attempt to emulate the more individualistic spontaneity of Caucasians, they sometimes see the latter as not carrying their share of the load in group situations and not being conscientious about repaying social obligations. Japanese Americans see the more individualistic white

115

Americans as having more limited social memories and are apt to judge their behavior as selfish.

In recent years, in some areas of the country, there has been a revival of Japanese American ethnic associations that focus on traditional Japanese cultural content. Frequently the Sansei, like the third generation European ethnics, are more comfortable about their ethnicity than were their parents, and thus they can return, oftentimes in a somewhat romantic way, to traditional cultural practices abandoned by the Nisei. This is seen, for example, in the Jan Ken Po summer school in Sacramento to which the Sansei send their children (Yonsei) to be exposed to Japanese language, foods, and religions as well as cultural forms such as judo, kendo, and calligraphy.

Nonetheless, it would appear that by and large the associations which remain most critical for community cohesion are those which combine mainstream cultural content with an opportunity for Japanese Americans to interact with one another with a distinct yet comfortable set of interactional rules.

THE ADAPTABILITY OF JAPANESE CULTURE

As noted earlier, one of the most distinctive features of Japanese culture has been its ability to incorporate elements of other cultures while retaining its most fundamental characteristic, the preservation of the group (e.g., Yamamoto and Wagatsuma 1980). By and large, specific cultural practices, such as religion, have been of secondary concern. At times, the Japanese have persecuted "alien" religious groups, as was the case with Christians during the seventeenth century, but their reaction was due more to the supposed damage these different belief systems might do to the homogeneity of the Japanese people than to any inherent "rightness" or "wrongness" of the beliefs themselves (e.g., Reischauer 1981, 68).

Because of this outlook, the Japanese have been extraordinarily successful in adopting useful elements of other cultures without suffering a loss to their own sense of unique peoplehood. Contrary to the sociological predictions of the time, the Japanese did not lose their identity as a unique people by adopting Western technology and dress following World War II. Indeed, just as they did during an earlier period when they adopted significant elements of Chi-

The Persistence of Community

nese culture, the Japanese used foreign cultural elements to enhance their own standing vis-à-vis other nations in the world (e.g., Reischauer 1981, 44–51, 228–230).

This adaptability might suggest a cultural relativism in which "anything goes" and everyone does his/her "own thing." This could not be further from the truth. As many observers have reported, the Japanese are among the most rule-guided people in the world. Rather, relativism in Japanese culture is defined in terms of group adaptation and survival. From a Western perspective, however, the Japanese often appear to incorporate and adapt incongruent cultural elements, such as when they practice multiple religions (e.g., Shintoism and Buddhism) or what they call multilayered faith. At its extreme, "ethics blends off into politeness and good manners" (Reischauer 1981, 143).

One example of how the Japanese penchant for "fitting in" has assisted Japanese Americans in reconciling traditional cultural demands and the demands of American society is found in the area of family and kinship ties. In Japanese culture, it is the men who represent their families to the outside world, including linking with the heads of related families. In the American context this would violate the cultural ideal of independent nuclear families. Given the importance of kin support among Japanese Americans, women in the Japanese American community have taken over the linking function, since they can do so in a more unobtrusive manner. In this way they retain the most important element of traditional Japanese culture, the preservation of the group, while not visibly violating mainstream American cultural ideals (Yanagisako 1977).

Japanese cultural flexibility, however, is not free of costs for the individual Japanese American. Although it would seem that such flexibility permits a person to live in both the ethnic and mainstream worlds to a greater extent than may be possible for those from other cultural traditions, it may also mean that s/he remains somewhat disconnected from both worlds. The sense of loneliness reported in Gehrie's (1976) study of the Sansei in Chicago may indeed be a warning of what increasing numbers of Sansei and Yonsei (fourth generation) may face as they become more dispersed and move away from the cultural and social support networks found on the West Coast and in Hawaii.

SIX

THE FUTURE OF
JAPANESE AMERICANS

 In the last two chapters we described the unique position of Japanese Americans today. On the one hand, they exhibit fairly high levels of structural assimilation into the mainstream of American society: they live in white neighborhoods, work in mostly professional and managerial occupations, and intermarry at a substantial rate with majority group members. On the other hand, the community appears to be very resilient in its ability to persist in spite of its members' movement out of ethnic enclaves in the cities or rural areas. The critical question, then, is what is the likelihood that this pattern can continue very far into the future? Will there be, for example, any major shifts in the processes of structural assimilation and/or those related to the preservation of ethnic community life?

Our general thesis is that structural assimilation is likely to continue and that it will increase the likelihood that younger Japanese Americans will become increasingly concerned with the "symbolic" aspects of ethnicity, but that other factors, both external and internal to the group, will continue to maintain high levels of individual participation in ethnic community affairs. Of particular importance with respect to the latter, we will argue, are international events.

STRUCTURAL ASSIMILATION AND SYMBOLIC ETHNICITY

The reader will recall from our discussion in chapter 4 that the current intermarriage rate of Japanese Americans is quite high, approximating sixty percent of all new marriages (Kitano et al.

118

1984), but that its full impact has not yet been felt because of the low levels of intermarriage in the first and second generations. Thus, we would expect that the impact of intermarriage on Japanese American ethnicity will become greater in subsequent generations. In addition, the number of Japanese Americans who live in areas which have high concentrations of fellow ethnic group members is likely to further diminish. As the increasing number of educated professionals and managers make career-related moves, more and more of them will end up in places outside of Hawaii and the West Coast. This dispersion process, in turn, is likely to continue to increase the amount of contact they have with Caucasians as well as with other minorities.

Even on the West Coast, the present level of contact between Japanese Americans and Caucasians is quite high. This is illustrated in a recent study which compared levels of segregation and how they would affect the likelihood of contact between blacks, Asians, and Hispanics on the one hand and Caucasians on the other. The researchers' comparison of the situation of blacks and Asians in the San Francisco Bay Area is especially revealing:

A good place to begin is with the San Francisco SMSA, in which each group [i.e., blacks and Asians] constitutes about 11% of the population and each is associated with one or more enclave area. Blacks constitute about 24% of the population in the cities of San Francisco and Oakland, and 6% in the suburbs, yielding a probability of black-Anglo contact of .242 in the former and .398 in the latter. Thus, in spite of the fact that blacks are a very small part of the suburban population, they have only a 40% chance of living near non-Hispanic whites.

In contrast, Asians constitute 7% of the suburban population but have an Anglo-contact probability of .668. Within the central cities, in which they are 17% of the population, the probability of Anglo contact is .465. In San Francisco, of course, Asians are more concentrated than anywhere else in the continental United States. Even under conditions most conducive to spatial isolation, therefore, Asians have an almost 50–50 chance of living near Anglos. In fact, the probability of Asian contact with Anglos in San Francisco and Oakland *exceeds* the probability of contact with other Asians. The Asian-Asian contact probability is only .314 in these central cities, and .128 in their suburbs. . . . Asians are more likely to reside near Anglos than near other Asians in cities or suburbs [Massey and Denton 1988, 608].

The likelihood that Japanese Americans will become even more widely dispersed throughout white middle-class neighborhoods suggests that they will be more likely to develop friendships with their majority group neighbors as well as intermarry with them. Our survey data in California show a very consistent pattern whereby Japanese Americans in areas with relatively low concentrations of fellow ethnics are more likely to have at least one best friend who is white, to have a Caucasian spouse, and to participate in nonethnic voluntary associations (see Fugita and O'Brien 1991).

An important question for the future is, if the trend toward structural assimilation continues will it also mean that Japanese Americans will become more like the third generation of other immigrant ethnic groups, essentially moving away from active involvement in ethnic community associations and turning toward a mainly symbolic concern with ethnicity as part of their personal identities?

Herbert Gans (1979) has pointed out that as individuals become structurally assimilated they become less dependent on their respective ethnic communities to meet their daily needs. Thus, first generation immigrants are forced to depend on one another for work, friendship, and finding marriage partners. But as successive generations become more acculturated and acceptable to the majority group, they find jobs alongside of majority group persons, form friendships with nonethnics, and eventually are more likely to marry persons of other backgrounds. Being less dependent on fellow ethnics, Gans goes on to say, they turn their attention away from ethnicity as a means of meeting material needs and instead begin to focus on ethnicity as an important part of their personal identity. Speaking of the experiences of the third generation of European immigrant groups, Gans observes that this shift from daily involvement in an ethnic community to a concern with "symbolic" aspects of ethnicity means that individuals will

> look for easy and intermittent ways of expressing their identity, for ways that do not conflict with other ways of life. As a result, they refrain from ethnic behavior that requires an arduous or time-consuming commitment, either to a culture that must be practiced constantly, or to organizations that demand active membership. Second, because people's concern is with identity, rather than with cultural

practices or group relationships, they are free to look for ways of expressing that identity which suit them best, thus opening up the possibility of voluntary, diverse or individualistic ethnicity. Any mode of expressing ethnic identity is valid as long as it enhances the feeling of being ethnic, and any cultural pattern or organization which nourishes that feeling is therefore relevant, providing only that enough people make the same choice when identity expression is a group enterprise. [1979, 8–9]

Moreover, symbolic ethnicity is a sign that the group has achieved enough acceptance and political power that they no longer feel that they have to prove that they are "real" Americans. For this reason, symbolic ethnicity can be very dramatic and colorful. It is this type which was most characteristic of the so-called ethnic revival among third generation European ethnics during the 1970s (Gans 1979).

As Japanese Americans become more structurally assimilated we would expect that they, like Americans of European origins, will become more concerned with developing a heightened sense of symbolic ethnicity. The most important current stimulus to the development of a more visible symbolic ethnicity among Japanese Americans has been the successful campaign to obtain redress from the U.S. government for the wartime incarceration. From one point of view, the effectiveness of this campaign is testimony to the commitment, persistence, and cooperation of thousands of Japanese Americans who contributed in various individual and organizational capacities. Although in the early stages of the movement there was considerable disagreement (and apathy) about the wisdom of pursuing redress, eventually almost all segments of the community came to support it.

At the same time, however, the success of the redress campaign is also evidence that Japanese Americans, as a group, have become firmly entrenched in the mainstream of American society. Although many persons and interest groups outside of the ethnic community supported redress for moral reasons, the fact that Japanese Americans now have greater access to persons in powerful political and economic positions was critical to the cause. The group is no longer the isolated and powerless minority which was rounded up and thrown into camps in 1942. In this respect they are similar to many European ethnic groups who now have the resources and security to be assertive about their ethnicity (Novak 1972).

In fact, Japanese Americans may have some advantages over other immigrant ethnic groups with respect to building and maintaining the symbolic bases of their ethnicity since the wartime internment provides such a clear-cut and emotionally laden set of events. In this regard, they are similar to groups like Armenian Americans or Jewish Americans which have a dramatic set of events, such as the Turkish massacre of the Armenians or the Holocaust, respectively, on which to focus their ethnic symbols.

In the case of Japanese Americans, the symbolic value of the incarceration continues to be amplified because the Sansei generation came of age during the late 1960s and early 1970s when the ethnic revival and the various black and Chicano cultural movements were taking place. Proclaiming one's "roots" is now much easier and more positively evaluated by society as a whole. This departs markedly from earlier periods when the "melting pot" ideology was dominant (e.g., Hofstadter 1955a).

Recently there has been a marked increase in the development of museums and historical societies designed to promote an understanding of the Japanese American experience. The National Japanese American Historical Society, the National Japanese American Museum, the Japanese American Library, and the Smithsonian exhibit on the wartime incarceration provide very tangible support for symbolic ethnicity.

The development that may have the strongest long-run impact on creation and preservation of the symbols of Japanese and other Asian American ethnicity is the institutionalization of Asian American studies programs. During the late 1960s and throughout the 1970s a number of these centers were established, along with other ethnic studies programs, on West Coast college campuses, reluctantly funded in response to the tumult associated with student demands for a more "relevant" curriculum dealing with "real world" problems.

Given that they were created under pressure and generally were resisted by faculty and administrators, it is not surprising that these centers have tried to mobilize Asian Americans along left-of-center ideological lines. Nevertheless, they have had a significant impact on a much wider range of Japanese American, as well as other Asian American, college students. Because these programs are a major source of writings about ethnic community history as well as contemporary issues, they have also helped to create a greater concern with ethnicity in the Japanese American community as a whole.

Asian American studies programs are currently undergoing some growing pains; their reasons for being have shifted in response to changes in the social and economic composition of the Asian American population and in society at large. Especially important here has been the heavy influx of immigrants from Southeast Asia, Korea, Taiwan, Hong Kong, and the Philippines. The more acculturated Chinese American, Japanese American, and Filipino American students who originally started the Asian American centers were most interested in symbolic identity issues and impacting the political system. Recent immigrants, more concerned with basic economic well-being, find some of the symbols of the Asian American movement removed from their more practical, day-to-day struggles. Their primary goal is to succeed in the mainstream of American economic life. Further, the current conservative mood of the country at large has allowed the universities to withdraw resources from these programs and to require their academic personnel to conform to more traditional academic activities and standards.

Even within the older Asian American ethnic groups, including Japanese Americans, there are cleavages which create obstacles in the search for symbols to link together the various groups and subgroups. Within the Japanese American community, the life experiences of second generation Nisei are vastly different from those of the third generation Sansei who were part of the student group which pushed for the Asian American studies programs. Older Japanese Americans can relate easily to the purposes of traditional academic departments since they are associated with their concern with upward mobility for themselves and their children. Some of the earlier rhetoric of the Asian American studies programs was seen by persons in the older generation as at best a little strange and at worst subversive.

The early appeals of professors and students to link the struggles of Asian Americans with those of the Third World, for example, seemed inexplicable and threatening to many older Japanese Americans who were brought up to believe that the best way to succeed in America is through quiet perseverance (e.g., Fugita and O'Brien 1977). In many respects, these intergenerational ideological differences are fairly typical of what has occurred in other immigrant ethnic groups in the United States (e.g., Novak 1972). Over the past decade, however, these ideological differences have become more muted, as they have in the country as a whole. Evidence of this is found in the fact that the two generations effectively worked together on the redress campaign.

In any event, it is clear that we should expect to find an increase in the development of symbolic aspects of Japanese American ethnicity as well as heightened visibility of Asian American ethnicity in general. Nevertheless, while the persistence of this type of ethnicity may be a source of great psychological satisfaction to future generations, it does not tell us whether Japanese American community life will continue in its present form. Will it be true, as suggested by Gans (1979), that this "easier" form of ethnicity necessarily means the demise of the more "difficult" types of ethnic involvement, particularly participation in ethnic community associations?

THE PERSISTENCE OF ETHNIC COMMUNITY INSTITUTIONS

Our survey in California shows that the dispersion of the Japanese American population into white neighborhoods does not necessarily have a negative effect on the desire and/or ability of persons in the ethnic community to interact with one another (see also Fugita and O'Brien 1991, Oguri-Kendis 1979). The most significant finding in this regard is that although those living in areas with a smaller number of fellow ethnics are more likely to interact socially with Caucasians than those living in "ethnic ghettos," they are no less likely to maintain membership in Japanese American voluntary associations. Indeed, the level of membership in ethnic associations was substantially higher in those areas where the ethnic population was relatively low. Apparently, when Japanese Americans find themselves in areas where they are a relatively small proportion of the population, they will make an extra effort to create formal organizations to maintain ethnic community ties

(Fugita and O'Brien 1991; O'Brien and Fugita 1983b; Oguri-Kendis 1979).

It should be noted, however, that the areas in the survey with relatively small proportions of Japanese Americans *in relation to the total population* (somewhat more than 1% of the populations in Fresno and Sacramento) still contained a sufficient number of ethnic group members to support a variety of Japanese American organizations, such as churches and social clubs. There may very well be a point at which the ethnic population becomes so small that it is unable to support much in the way of voluntary associational life at all. It is clear, for example, that midwestern metropolitan areas with substantially smaller absolute numbers of Japanese Americans than even the low ethnicity density areas in our West Coast study have a more difficult time getting people to take the time and effort to keep ethnic associations viable (see Albert 1980; Fugita and Tanaka 1987). This will be more of a concern in the future as greater numbers of Japanese Americans move away from Hawaii and the West Coast.

Nonetheless, the apparent resourcefulness of the Japanese American community in finding ways to maintain organizational life in the face of the rapid dispersal of the population following World War II suggests that geographical and ecological factors in themselves will not pose an insurmountable obstacle. This is particularly true for the Nisei who have shared so many life experiences (O'Brien and Fugita 1983b). The more serious threat to the persistence of a vibrant ethnic community, in our view, will come from the effects of the increased rates of intermarriage.

Japanese Americans who marry Caucasians are less likely than those who marry within the ethnic group to participate actively in the ethnic community. This is seen, for example, in a comparison of the proportion in each group which belongs to ethnic voluntary associations. While over three-quarters (78%) of the Sansei who are married to Japanese Americans belong to at least one Japanese American organization, only half of those Sansei who are married to Caucasians participate in the same way (Fugita, O'Brien, and Kooney 1984). At the same time, however, it should be pointed out that the level of participation of the intermarried is still ten times higher than that found in studies of the involvement of Italian and Irish Americans in their respective ethnic communities (Goering

1971; Roche 1982). Thus, even with changes in the geographical distribution and intermarriage rate of Japanese Americans it is likely that there will continue to exist a Japanese American community which can rely on the contributions of its members to collective goals.

The exact shape of the ethnic community in the future is more difficult to predict. The greatest obstacle in this regard, of course, is our inability to predict dramatic changes in factors external to the group itself. Who, for example, in the mid-1930s would have predicted the attack on Pearl Harbor and the subsequent internment of Japanese Americans in concentration camps? It is equally unlikely that many, either inside or outside of the ethnic community, could have foreseen the high degree of acceptance of Japanese Americans by most white Americans following the war.

Nevertheless, with these reservations in mind, it appears that two sets of factors outside the control of Japanese Americans are likely to have a substantial impact on the character of their ethnic community in the future. The first of these is the ascendancy of Japan and the Pacific Rim countries in recent decades. The second is the substantial increase in migration from Asia. Although only a tiny minority of these immigrants are from Japan, the dramatic increase in the economic power of Asians overseas coupled with the equally dramatic increase in the numbers and resources of Asians in America is likely to have profound consequences for the viability and direction of Japanese American ethnic institutions. By and large, we expect that these factors will create a more assertive ethnic community, and one which will increasingly form political coalitions with other Asian American groups, but, at the same time, a community which will experience more instances of hostility from resentful whites than would have been the case even a decade ago.

THE PACIFIC RIM ECONOMIC BOOM AND ASIAN IMMIGRATION

The world is now approaching what some have dubbed "the Pacific Century." The economic and political developments underway in the Pacific Rim countries are no less than monumental. The growth of the post–World War II Japanese economy, and more recently that of Korea, Taiwan, Hong Kong, and Singapore, has not only realigned world markets and political relationships but has directly impacted on the daily lives of ordinary people throughout the world. Much of this development is positive. From an American perspective, not only have several key trading partners been very substantially strengthened but Americans have come to enjoy and rely upon the high value and technologically advanced consumer products which have poured out of these countries.

Japan's rapid postwar economic development and the by and large friendly relations between that nation and the United States has made it a more attractive country for Japanese Americans to claim as their ancestral homeland. This has stimulated an increased interest and pride in their cultural origins. Nevertheless, some older people in the ethnic community would still like to distance themselves from Japan. Beckman (1989) has recently warned Hawaii's Japanese American community to dissociate themselves from things Japanese because with the rise in competition between the U.S. and Japan, U.S. nationalism could once again fail to distinguish between Japanese and Japanese Americans.

The emergence of the Pacific Rim countries, especially Japan, as economic powers has not only resulted in new sources of tension and potential conflict for Americans as a whole but also created some special problems for Japanese Americans. While scholars, politicians, and the general public may debate whether the success of the new Asian economic powers is due to their efficient social arrangements and their work ethic or to their "cheap labor" and unfair trade practices, the critical fact for Japanese Americans and other Asian Americans is that resentment generated by this new competitiveness is very likely to spill over to them personally.

In recent years there has been an increasing amount of hostility toward Asians in America. Not only have displaced automobile production workers had Toyota bashing parties, but we have witnessed high status influentials, such as Michigan Congressman John Dingell, talking about "little yellow people."

Even though many businessmen have studied and copied the techniques of the Japanese, the anxiety which has been a byproduct of the increased economic competition between the two nations has brought to the surface some subtle and latent biases which normally would have remained hidden. The purchase of significant amounts of visible real estate in Hawaii and major mainland cities by overseas Japanese has further exacerbated this situation (Zinsmeister 1987).

Another direct source of conflict affecting Japanese Americans has been the heavy influx of new Asian immigrants during the past two decades. This is principally the product of two developments: political instabilities in the Far East and changes in our immigration laws. Some unfortunate byproducts of this, however, have been feuds between white and Vietnamese shrimpers in Texas and rock-throwing melees involving Southeast Asian immigrants and working class whites and blacks in Massachusetts.

According to the Justice Department, there was a 62 percent increase in anti-Asian incidents from 1984 to 1985. In Los Angeles County, Asians were the target of 50 percent of the racial incidents in 1986. In Boston, where the number of Asian Americans is minuscule, 29 percent of the racial crimes recorded by the police were committed against members of these ethnic groups (Zinsmeister 1987).

Unlike most other Asian groups, the Japanese are not immigrating to this country in significant numbers at this time. Only about 5,000 enter the United States as immigrants each year. A substantial and increasing number of Japanese businessmen and their families, however, are on temporary duty in the U.S., particularly in Southern California. Very few of them permanently settle in this country. Nevertheless, their highly visible affluence further fuels the resentments of white Americans toward Asians, including some Japanese Americans. A substantial proportion of Japanese Americans feel that the Japanese nationals are arrogant and that their behavior will cause them (i.e., Japanese Americans) to have to endure negative reactions from the American public (Suomisto 1988).

Moreover, a fact of life for Japanese Americans is that unlike the third generation of European immigrant groups, they can never blend into the society simply by adopting middle class dress, manners, and language. Asians will always "look different," unless, of course, they intermarry with whites.

As we have noted, the intermarriage rate has increased dramatically among Japanese Americans since the end of World War II. Yet those children who are the offspring of two Asian parents are still seen as "foreigners" by many Americans. It is likely that they will be targets of resentment, at least for the foreseeable future, and be buffeted by tensions associated with international events.

Because Japanese Americans physically resemble the new Asian immigrants, they are often treated as if they are a part of this "new wave." Thus, whether they accept the newly created Asian American political identity or not, in many ways they cannot avoid its effects. This issue may generate increasing controversy within the ethnic community. Because different cohorts of Japanese Americans have had different historical experiences they are likely to interpret increasing tensions between the United States and Japan in different ways. This makes it difficult to define an "ethnic position" on the problem.

The well publicized success of Asians and Asian Americans who look, and sometimes act, "different" threatens many whites who see themselves as representative of the "mainstream" of American life. At a recent community meeting in Redondo Beach, California, a local resident blurted out, "Those damn people own the country." In Silver Lake, an affluent section of Los Angeles, two white men sarcastically confronted two Asian men inside a fashionable restaurant with "Where's the Honda convention? Where's the camera?" They had to be ejected by restaurant employees (Torres 1988). One-quarter of those responding to a recent *Los Angeles Times* poll agreed with the statement: "Asians are gaining too much power." No other group was seen as such a threat by more than 7 percent of the respondents. Also telling was that some 44 percent of the Anglos interviewed said that they resent seeing foreign languages used in store signs (*Asian Week* 1989). A common stereotype of Asians is that they are "driven workaholics" who do not want to adopt the "American way of life." The director of the Vietnamese Fishermen Association in Oakland, California, explained that "they don't go in for a beer. They don't go in to watch football. That makes other people mad" (Zinsmeister 1987).

Perhaps the greatest amount of tension in recent years has been between Asian shopkeepers and black inner-city residents. Most of these entrepreneurs are recent immigrants who typically have college degrees but are unable to use them in professional pursuits because of language or licensing problems. If they had their "druthers," the shopkeepers would be doing something else and most certainly would be working in a safer middle class environment. Inner-city residents are apt to see the Asian entrepreneurs as simply another in a long list of groups that have come into their community to exploit them (Kim, Hurh, and Fernandez 1988).

The kinds of tensions just described can sometimes erupt into violent confrontations. Recently in Washington, D.C., the owner of a Chinese-American takeout restaurant chased a black woman patron out of his establishment with an unregistered handgun. Rev. Willie Wilson, leader of the subsequent boycott against the restaurant, proclaimed, "The Asian community is the latest of a series of ethnic groups that have come into our community, disrespected us, raped us economically, and moved out at our expense" (Zinsmeister 1987).

Asian shopkeepers generally respond to such charges with the claim that they are simply trying to make a living and indeed are giving up a lot by working long hours at relatively low rates of remuneration (Zinsmeister 1987). The historical relationship between nonresident shopkeepers and blacks in the inner city is, of course, an old one that was in place many years before the Asian immigrants arrived. Nonetheless, it remains a continual source of friction and ill will.

Another area of tension between Asian Americans and other Americans, including both whites and other minorities, which impacts on Japanese Americans is that of admission to prestigious colleges and universities. An example of an attitude held by some whites on such campuses is found in graffiti scribbled on the wall of a UCLA student union men's room, "UCLA, University for Caucasians, Lots of Asians."

During the late 1960s and early 1970s, Asian Americans were viewed by many as an underrepresented minority group which should be given preference in admissions to colleges and universities. This has dramatically changed; Asians are usually overrepresented, relative to their proportions in the general population, on many elite university campuses such as those in the University of California system and the Ivy League. They comprise, for example, about 37 percent of the freshman class at UCLA and 20 percent at Harvard. Incidentally, the latter figure is still a lower representation than is found among Jews, who comprise between 25 and 30 percent of the student bodies in many Ivy League schools (Zinsmeister 1987).

At Harvard, which was cited by the Supreme Court in the Bakke decision (a case in which the court ruled against the University of California system for "reverse discrimination" against whites) as having a model affirmative action program, university officials concede that Asians have a lower admission rate than whites. They claim that this is a result of Asians scoring lower on athletic ability and having fewer alumni/alumnae as parents. These criteria, the officials point out, are used to insure "diversity" in their student body. Advocates for Asians, however, charge that such practices are merely an updated version of the quotas used earlier by Harvard to discriminate against Jewish applicants (Oren 1985; Synnott 1979; Tsuang 1989). They note, for example, that Asian American applicants to Harvard do have somewhat higher SAT scores (about 50 points when the verbal and math sections are combined) than other applicants. At the University of California, critics have complained that admissions criteria have been changed to place greater weight on extracurricular activities, compared with academic criteria, specifically to reduce the number of Asians admitted.

There is also evidence of discrimination against Japanese Americans in higher level managerial and professional positions (Cabezas and Kawaguchi 1988; Woodrum 1981) as well as a general perception by persons in this ethnic community that they are still potential targets of discrimination, both economically and socially (O'Brien and Fugita 1983a). Some have labeled the exclusion of Asians from the top rungs of corporate and government hierarchies as the "glass ceiling" (Lyons 1989).

All of the sources of tension described above have increased the defensive reactions of Asian Americans as a whole. Not only have these tensions raised the significance of ethnicity for them but they also have provided a strong incentive to create and maintain organizations which will be able to protect and otherwise advance the interests of the group in the political arena.

Moreover, Japanese Americans, like most Americans, have adopted more exacting standards with regard to discrimination and their civil rights. They also have more resources within their community with which to protect their rights. There are, for example, many Sansei lawyers who are willing to contribute their talents to pursue collective community goals. This was demonstrated by the long hours spent preparing legal documents during the redress movement. In addition, the greater assimilation of Japanese Americans has markedly increased their ability to make contact with influentials outside of the group and this, of course, has boosted their political influence. Finally, the dramatic increase in the size of the many Asian American communities has made possible the development of effective political coalitions. The lure of increased political clout will provide an additional incentive for Asian Americans to emphasize ethnicity.

There are now a number of influential Japanese American public officials, such as the former chair of the Iran-Contra committee, Senator Daniel Inouye. In addition, the election of Japanese Americans to public office in areas where they are a small minority is evidence that the political resources of their community now go beyond the ethnic group itself. This is seen, for example, in the elections of Congressmen Norman Mineta of Pleasanton (near San Jose) and Robert Matsui of Sacramento, both of whom ran in districts with relatively small numbers of Japanese Americans.

UNIQUENESS AND FLEXIBILITY IN JAPANESE AMERICAN CULTURE

It is appropriate in this final section of the book to return to the theme with which we started: that is, that although various kinds of "structural constraints" may pose new challenges, Japanese Americans have a culture which is capable of responding effectively to change. Much to the surprise of some observers, and perhaps even to Japanese Americans themselves, they were able to go through enormous hardships in building farms and businesses in areas of California which were seen by many as unfit for production, only to suffer a cruel incarceration and the attendant loss of their material gains, experience a radical restructuring of the authority and direction of the ethnic community itself, and finally emerge in the postwar decades firmly entrenched in the mainstream of American life. At the same time, again in contrast to conventional scholarly wisdom, Japanese Americans have managed to retain a vibrant community which in one sense looks much different than it did two generations ago, but in another sense bears some remarkable signs of continuity.

The continuity in the Japanese American community is based on a culture which defines human relationships in such a way that individuals feel a sense of obligation to participate in activities which will promote the persistence and success of the group. In the early years in California this meant the development and maintenance of an ethnic economy that depended on considerable cooperation and trust among its participants. In the internment camps, it meant the willingness of significant numbers of persons to continue to work together even though the traditional authority structure of the community was torn asunder. It would have been very easy, by any human standard, for individuals to have been consumed by resentment over their unjust treatment and to become totally demoralized. In the postwar period it has meant the willingness of members of the group who no longer need the ethnic community for their economic livelihood to continue to find rewards in interacting with one another, "pulling their weight" in order to keep their associations, whether they be golf clubs, churches, the JACL, or housing for the aged Issei, going strong.

It is clear that the "programming" of Japanese Americans toward a more group-centered view of human relationships occurs quite early in life and has been passed down from one generation to the next. The roots of these principles, as we showed earlier, are found in many centuries of Japanese culture (e.g., Yamamoto and Wagatsuma 1980). The key to their strength is precisely their ability to adapt to a wide variety of circumstances and especially to drastic changes in what the Japanese would see as fairly superficial cultural content. Perhaps here is a clue to the difficulty faced in so many of our groups in the larger society which focus on specific, and oftentimes superficial, cultural content, while placing the survival and health of the group in at best a secondary position.

Furthermore, it would seem, as Miyamoto (1986–87) points out, that the high degree of sensitivity to the feelings of others and focusing on group needs means that Japanese Americans operate on a "different gear ratio" than most Caucasian Americans. Although their high degree of structural assimilation attests to the fact that they can interact effectively with Caucasians in the work world and in many kinds of interpersonal situations, there is considerable evidence that they still find social encounters with fellow ethnics more comfortable in many ways (O'Brien and Fugita 1983a).

In the past, as succeeding generations of Japanese Americans became more structurally assimilated, they came closer to adopting mainstream values with respect to individual choice and personal autonomy (Connor 1977, 308). At the same time, however, there has been considerable retention of traditional Japanese approaches to interpersonal relations. One of the reasons why Japanese Americans have retained many of the characteristics of the Japanese interpersonal style in the ethnic community and family is that there has been little pressure to give them up in these settings. Because of the sensitivity of Japanese culture to social contexts, however, they are generally able to make the transition to mainstream social settings quite well.

One scholar who has studied three generations of Japanese Americans in Sacramento concludes that the third generation Sansei still "are more deferent, more abasive, less dominant, more affiliative, less aggressive, and have a greater need for succorance and order than do the Sacramento State University Caucasian students" (Connor 1977, 305). Other studies show that despite a substantial decline in adherence to many traditional Japanese cultural practices as well as a loss of facility with the Japanese language, there is a great deal of continuity between generations in basic psychological outlook toward relating to self and others (e.g., Johnson 1976; O'Brien and Fugita 1983a). Thus, the retention of "Japaneseness" has been selective and new forms of ethnicity have emerged (Miyamoto 1986–87; Yanagisako 1985).

Given the persistence of these characteristics in the face of high levels of structural assimilation, there would seem to be little reason to expect that they will disappear soon. These deeply ingrained attitudes and feelings about interpersonal relations will play a key role in preserving the network of voluntary associations which have served to formally keep persons and families in the community tied to one another. The fact that Japanese Americans have grown up and feel most comfortable in an interpersonal context which is qualitatively different than that found in most other social settings in America, reinforces their sense of "differentness." Moreover, if social and economic discrimination against them increases in response to international events, it will provide an increased incentive for them to seek out ethnic organizational settings in which they not only are safe from subtle forms of prejudice but also experience a positive affirmation of self. It will also tend to reinforce those incentives, noted earlier, to use newly found political resources to gain advantages for the group.

A second reason why the culture that guides the way Japanese Americans relate to one another is likely to continue to play a major role in encouraging ethnic community cohesion is that it remains a very effective way of organizing people, irrespective of cultural background or interests. Quite simply, those who are predisposed to work together over long periods of time and seek collective over individual goals are more likely to be successful in forming and maintaining organizations than those with highly individualistic bents. Indeed, the group-centered Japanese approach to organizational survival has received a good deal of positive treatment in American management circles in recent years because many aspects of it work even in an American context (Ouchi 1984).

Moreover, Japanese Americans currently have an advantage common to all ethnic groups with extensive networks of voluntary associations, which one sociologist terms "organizational momentum" (Reitz 1980, 216). Even though the initial reasons for starting ethnic associations may have long passed, as in the case of the mutual aid societies referred to earlier, they will frequently adapt to meet new needs or simply create a new set of incentives with which to retain the involvement of their members. Reitz observes:

Once an organization is created, it will tend to maintain itself and the group it represents because it satisfies a new set of social interests on its own and thus generates a set of social opportunities. Those who have jobs in an organization, those who enjoy the prestige of organization leadership and those who have found, in an ethnic club, a satisfying means of community involvement may find they have strong interests in maintaining the organization (in addition to their identification with explicit goals of the organization). Organizations may provide all sorts of social opportunities, which are only weakly related to their initial purpose. This supports their survival. Organizations create their own social momentum by reinforcing informal (traditional) beliefs and social patterns. In fact, organizations frequently outlast the needs they were originally intended to serve. To maintain their constituency, they lead or facilitate the search for new needs. [1980, 216]

As we saw earlier, one of the striking features of Japanese American associational life has been its ability to adapt to the changing needs and interests of succeeding generations. The content of groups like bowling, fishing, and golf clubs, professional, singles, or service associations seemingly has very little to do with traditional Japanese culture, and scarcely a word of Japanese, except expletives and euphemisms, may be spoken in such groupings. Yet it is clear that the principle of organization, especially the group-centered interpersonal environment, is a product of the same cultural legacy that helped the Issei immigrants organize collective production and marketing arrangements in their ethnic agricultural economy.

Ironically, in an era in which middle class white Americans are discovering the limits of an isolated individualism (e.g., Lasch 1979) and the need to "network" and create support groups, Japanese Americans are able to call upon their traditional ways of social organization which in earlier times frequently were seen as unfair and indeed un-American. Thus, it would seem, as other observers have noted, not only that Japanese American ethnicity is alive and well but that the core culture of American society may in fact be moving a few degrees toward it. If that is true, then we should have even more reason to expect that Japanese Americans will feel quite comfortable participating actively in both their ethnic community and the mainstream of American life.

APPENDIXES

Population of Chinese, Japanese, Blacks, and Caucasians
in the U.S., 1870–1980

Year	All Races	Chinese	Japanese	Blacks	Caucasians
1980	226,545,805	806,040	700,974	26,495,025	188,371,622
		(0.4%)	(0.3%)	(11.7%)	(83.1%)
1970	203,211,926	435,062	591,290	22,580,289	177,748,975
		(0.2%)	(0.3%)	(11.1%)	(87.5%)
1960	179,323,175	237,292	464,332	18,871,831	158,831,732
		(0.1%)	(0.3%)	(10.5%)	(88.6%)
1950	151,325,798	150,005	326,379	15,044,937	135,149,629
		(0.1%)	(0.2%)	(9.9%)	(89.3%)
1940	132,165,129	106,334	285,115	12,865,914	118,357,831
		(0.1%)	(0.2%)	(9.7%)	(89.6%)
1930	123,202,660	102,159	278,743	11,891,842	110,395,253
		(0.1%)	(0.2%)	(9.7%)	(89.6%)
1920	106,021,568	85,202	220,596	10,463,607	94,903,540
		(0.1%)	(0.2%)	(9.9%)	(89.5%)
1910	92,228,531	94,414	152,745	9,828,667	81,812,405
		(0.1%)	(0.1%)	(10.7%)	(88.7%)
1900	76,212,168	118,746	85,716	8,834,395	66,809,196
		(0.2%)	(0.1%)	(11.6%)	(87.7%)
1890	62,947,714	107,488	2,039	7,488,676	55,101,258
		(0.2%)	(0.003%)	(11.9%)	(87.5%)
1880	50,155,783	105,465	148	6,580,793	43,402,970
		(0.2%)	(0.0003%)	(13.1%)	(86.5%)
1870	38,558,371	63,199	55	4,880,009	33,589,377
		(0.2%)	(0.0001%)	(12.7%)	(87.1%)

SOURCES: U.S. Bureau of the Census 1975, 14; U.S. Bureau of the Census 1983b, table 40.

Appendixes

**Percentage Distribution of Persons of Chinese, Japanese,
and Caucasian Ancestry by Regions, 1980**

Region	Chinese (812,178)	Japanese (716,331)	Caucasian (189,035,012)
Northeast	26.8	6.5	22.5
Midwest	9.2	6.5	27.7
South	11.3	6.6	31.3
West	52.7	80.3	18.6

SOURCE: U.S. Bureau of the Census 1983c, table 232.

APPENDIX 3

Immigrants, by Region, 1961–1984 (in thousands)

Country of Birth	1961–1970	1971–1980	1981–1983	1984
All Countries	3,321.7	4,493.3	1,750.5	543.9
Asia	445.3	1,633.8	855.3	256.3
China*	96.7	202.5	105.3	35.8
Hong Kong	25.6	47.5	15.0	5.5
India	31.2	176.8	68.7	25.0
Iran	10.4	46.2	32.6	13.8
Iraq	6.4	23.4	8.0	2.9
Israel	12.9	26.6	10.1	3.1
Japan	38.5	47.9	11.9	4.0
Jordan	14.0	29.6	9.5	2.4
Korea	35.8	272.0	97.7	33.0
Lebanon	7.5	33.8	10.4	3.2
Philippines	101.5	360.2	130.4	42.8
Thailand	5.0	44.1	16.2	4.9
Turkey	6.8	18.6	7.9	1.8
Vietnam	4.6	179.7	165.7	37.2
Europe	1,238.6	801.3	194.7	64.1
North America	1,351.1	1,645.0	537.0	166.7
Canada	266.7	114.8	33.4	10.8
Mexico	443.3	637.2	216.5	57.6
Caribbean	519.5	759.8	214.0	74.3
Central America	97.7	132.4	72.7	24.1
South America	228.3	284.4	107.4	37.5
Africa	39.3	91.5	44.4	15.5
Australia	9.9	14.3	3.9	1.3
New Zealand	3.7	5.3	1.9	.6
Other Countries	5.5	17.7	5.9	1.9

* Includes Taiwan

SOURCE: U.S. Bureau of the Census 1988, table 129.

Appendixes

**Percentage of Multiple Ancestry Reported by
Selected Ancestry Groups in the U.S., 1980**

Ancestry Group	Percent Multiple Ancestry
Asian Indian	10.0
Albanian	43.9
Armenian	26.8
Austrian	64.2
Chinese	15.3
Dutch	77.7
English	52.1
Filipino	20.8
French	76.2
German	63.5
Greek	35.8
Irish	74.3
Italian	43.5
Japanese	15.7
Korean	8.8
Polish	53.7
Ukranian	47.8

Source: U.S. Bureau of the Census 1983a, table 2.

Percentage Distribution of Employed Persons of Japanese Ancestry by Major Industry in the U.S., 1900–1980

	1900	1920	1930	1960	1970	1980
Total Number of Employed Persons*	71,219	57,903	54,230	192,537	265,570	382,534
Personal Services	20.3%	22.0%	22.2%	8.7%	6.8%	4.8%
Mining	0.2%	2.0%	1.3%	0.08%	0.2%	0.2%
Manufacturing	3.3%	11.8%	7.0%	16.6%	15.7%	14.3%
Agriculture, Fishing, and Forestry	62.7%	44.3%	45.2%	14.2%	7.4%	4.8%
Transportation and Communications	9.6%	7.4%	4.2%	3.9%	5.4%	6.8%
Trade, Finance, Insurance, Real Estate	2.1%	9.9%	16.0%	27.5%	31.6%	35.9%
Professional Services	0.3%	2.2%	3.6%	13.4%	19.9%	20.7%
Public Administration	0.02%	0.06%	0.1%	6.6%	7.9%	7.6%
Construction	1.1%	0.2%	0.3%	5.7%	5.1%	3.8%
Other and Unspecified	0.4%	0.1%	0.01%	3.3%	—	1.1%

* 1900–1930, age 10 and over; 1960, age 14 and over; 1970–1980, age 16 and over.

SOURCE: U.S. Bureau of the Census 1904, table 3; U.S. Bureau of the Census 1923, table 5; U.S. Bureau of the Census 1933, table 6; U.S. Bureau of the Census 1963, table 39; U.S. Bureau of the Census 1973, table 7; U.S. Bureau of the Census 1983c, table 162.

APPENDIX 6

Percentage Distribution of Employed Persons of Chinese Ancestry by Major Industry in the U.S., 1870–1980

	1870	1900	1920	1930	1960	1970	1980
Total Number of Employed Persons*	46,274	105,480	45,614	47,106	98,784	185,031	399,964
Personal Services	40.9%	51.2%	58.0%	47.0%	10.9%	7.1%	3.6%
Mining	36.9%	3.1%	0.3%	0.05%	0.1%	0.2%	0.3%
Manufacturing	8.2%	10.1%	9.3%	7.6%	14.0%	17.3%	20.3%
Agriculture, Fishing, and Forestry	8.0%	23.7%	11.1%	7.4%	1.2%	0.9%	0.6%
Transportation, Communications	3.6%	1.2%	1.8%	2.2%	3.5%	4.2%	5.3%
Trade, Finance, Insurance, Real Estate	1.7%	10.0%	16.4%	30.8%	41.8%	39.8%	41.2%
Professional Services	0.7%	0.7%	0.9%	2.2%	13.2%	21.2%	21.3%
Public Administration	0.05%	—	0.4%	0.2%	6.9%	6.3%	4.8%
Construction	—	—			1.9%	2.3%	1.9%
Other and Unspecified	—	—	1.8%	2.6%	6.5%	0.7%	0.7%

* 1870–1930, age 10 and over; 1960, age 14; 1970–1980, age 16 and over.
SOURCE: U.S. Bureau of the Census 1872, table 65; U.S. Bureau of the Census 1904, table 3; U.S. Bureau of the Census 1920, table 5; U.S. Bureau of the Census 1933, table 6; U.S. Bureau of the Census 1963, table 40; U.S. Bureau of the Census 1973, table 22; U.S. Bureau of the Census 1983c, table 162.

APPENDIX 7

Percentage Distribution of Employed Persons in the General Population in the U.S. by Industry, 1980

Total Number of Employed Persons (16 years of age and older)	97,639,355
Personal Services	3.2%
Mining	1.1%
Manufacturing	22.4%
Agriculture, Fishing, Forestry	3.0%
Transportation, Communications	7.3%
Trade, Finance, Insurance, Real Estate	30.6%
Professional Services	20.3%
Public Administration	5.3%
Construction	5.9%
Other and Unspecified	1.0%

SOURCE: U.S. Bureau of the Census 1983c, table 90.

APPENDIX 8

Mean and Median Household Income for Persons of Japanese and Chinese ancestry and for the General Population of the U.S., 1979

	Mean Household Income	Median Household Income
Chinese	$23,657	$19,561
Japanese	$25,923	$22,517
U.S. Population	$20,306	$16,841

SOURCE: U.S. Bureau of the Census 1983c, tables 92 and 164.

APPENDIX 9

Percentage of Persons 25 Years of Age and Older with Four or More Years of College in Different Population Groups, 1940–1980

	1940	1950	1960	1970	1980
Caucasian	4.9	6.4	8.1	11.3	17.4
Chinese	3.0	9.0	16.5	25.6	36.6
Japanese	5.0	7.3	9.9	15.9	26.4
U.S. Total	4.6	6.2	7.7	11.0	17.0

SOURCES: U.S. Bureau of the Census 1988, table 201; U.S. Bureau of the Census 1943, table 6; U.S. Bureau of the Census 1953, tables 11, 12; U.S. Bureau of the Census 1963, tables 21, 22; U.S. Bureau of the Census 1973, tables 3, 18; U.S. Bureau of the Census 1983c, table 160.

APPENDIX 10

Orientals in Hawaii in Government Positions in Relation to Adult Citizenship, 1920–1955

Year	Elected Officials		Appointed Officials		Adult Citizens	
	%Oriental	%Japanese	%Oriental	%Japanese	%Oriental	%Japanese
1910	0.0	0.0	0.0	0.0	3.1	0.3
1920	1.1	0.0	0.8	0.0	12.7	5.5
1930	5.5	2.2	4.1	1.6	23.9	15.3
1940	24.2	14.3	6.3	2.9	35.9	26.6
1950	37.4	25.3	17.5	10.0	48.2	34.7

SOURCE: Yamamoto 1959, 360.

Appendixes

APPENDIX 11

U.S. Census and WRA Enumerations of Japanese Farms
by Tenure Status of Operators, California, 1910–1942

Date	Owners	Tenants	Managers	Total
1910	233	1,547	36	1,816
1920	506	4,533	113	5,152
1930	560	1,580	1,616	3,756
1940	1,290	3,596	249	5,135
1942	1,703	3,195	10	4,908

SOURCES: For 1910 and 1920, U.S. Census, *Agriculture*, 1920, V (1922), p. 312; for 1930 and 1940, U.S. Census, *Agriculture*, 1940, III (1943), p. 224; for 1942, War Relocation Authority evacuee property records, cited in Adon Poli and Warren M. Engstrand, "Japanese Agriculture on the Pacific Coast," *Journal of Land and Public Utility Economics*, 21 (Nov. 1945), 355.

APPENDIX 12

Farm Acreage Operated by Japanese Owners
and Tenants, California, 1905–1942

Date	Acres owned (in 1,000s)	Acres rented or worked under annual labor contract (in 1,000s)	Total
1905	2	60	62
1913	27	255	282
1920	75	383	458
1922	51	280	330[1]
1925	42	266	308
1932	38	250	288
1942	69	163	232

[1] Discrepancy due to rounding.

SOURCES: Except for 1942, the original authority for all years is the Japanese Association of America, as cited by Kiichi Kanzaki, *California and the Japanese* (San Francisco, 1921), p. 55; Yamato Ichihashi, *Japanese in the United States* (Stanford, 1932), p. 193; Edward K. Strong, Jr., *Japanese in California* (Stanford, 1933), p. 138. For 1942, the original authority is the War Relocation Authority evacuee property records, cited in Adon Poli and Warren M. Engstrand, "Japanese Agriculture on the Pacific Coast," *Journal of Land and Public Utility Economics*, 21 (Nov. 1945), 355.

BIBLIOGRAPHIC ESSAY

The literature listed below is designed to provide the reader with more details about various aspects of the Japanese American experience. In making our selections we have avoided Japanese language sources as well as highly technical material.

Currently there is no periodical specifically devoted to the Japanese American experience. *Amerasia Journal*, published quarterly since 1971 by the UCLA Asian American Studies Center, is a multidisciplinary periodical that contains the largest number of articles on Japanese Americans. It also publishes annually a selected bibliography of the field. Two sources of books and other material on Japanese Americans are the Japanese American Curriculum Project (JACP) in San Mateo, California, and the Amerasia Bookstore in Little Tokyo, in Los Angeles. JACP was organized in 1969 by volunteers from the Japanese American community who wanted to make material on the incarceration available. Since then, they have expanded and are now the single largest source of Asian American literature, particularly curriculum material.

INTRODUCTION

A good first step in understanding the people of any American ethnic group is to gain some appreciation of their culture and historical experiences before their arrival in the New World. In the case of Japanese Americans, a broad historical overview of the meaning of Japanese "peoplehood" is helpful. For the general reader, one of the best of these is Reischauer (1981), a book that is very readable and that has the additional virtue of tying together the different historical periods in Japan in a fashion that helps one to understand not only the Japanese but Japanese Americans as well.

A more sociological discussion of the Japanese has been written by Nakane (1970). A good contemporary treatment of how Japanese culture and social structure facilitate acommodation to changing situations by emphasizing long-term relationships is found in Dore (1986), which illustrates, with specific reference to the textile industry, how the Japanese economy has been able to adjust with "flexible rigidities" to changing market conditions. Other readings that provide a good intuitive sense of the kinds of "world view" in Japanese culture include Zander's (1983) discussion of the meaning of "group" and individual in Japan, both historically and at the present time, as well as Haglund's (1984) succinct treatment of some major Japanese cultural elements. An extended comparison of Oriental and Occidental concepts of interpersonal relationships is

147

found in Hsu's work (1971; 1975). Some scholars take issue with the extent to which he draws similarities between Chinese and Japanese culture, but nonetheless the imagery which this anthropologist uses to convey differences between Eastern and Western thinking can be helpful in understanding the Japanese American experience.

Most of the immigrants came from rural Japanese villages. To get a sense of what these were like, the reader can examine Embree's (1939) and Yoder's (1936) works and Norbeck's (1972) description of voluntary associations in Japan.

Critical reviews of some of the biases in earlier treatments of Asian immigrants to the United States are found in Cheng (1976) and Daniels (1966). One of the most comprehensive bibliographies of scholarly English language works on Japanese American history is found in Ichioka (1976). Examples of the so-called model minority view of the Japanese American experience are found in Hosokawa (1969) and Peterson (1970). Critical responses by Asian Americans to this perspective are found in Gee (1976), Hurh and Kim (1986), and Osajima (1988). Finally, a highly readable overview of the experiences and culture of Japanese Americans from a second generation Nisei point of view is found in Kitano (1976).

1. THE EARLY YEARS

The classic scholarly treatment of the immigration of the Japanese to Hawaii and the continental United States is Ichihashi (1932). This work contains many statistical details on the characteristics of the immigrants. The more recent works of Moriyama (1984, 1985) provide information about the reasons for the "push" out of Japan and immigration to Hawaii.

Since the Hawaiian Japanese experience is quite different from that of the mainland, it has its own distinct, although relatively small, literature. Some useful sources are Fuchs (1961), Ogawa (1978), Kotani (1985), and Rogers and Izutsu (1980). The latter contains an insightful discussion of Japanese American families and their values.

A good place to start locating sources to compare the historical experiences of the Japanese and the Chinese is the bibliographical essay by Chan in Okihiro et al. (1988). A current treatment of the Chinese American experience is found in Tsai (1986). A helpful discussion of the reasons for the greater initial socioeconomic success of the Japanese as compared with the Chinese is provided by Nee and Wong (1985). The reader wishing to look at more detailed statistical comparisons between the two ethnic groups is advised to examine the U.S. Census sources referred to in Appendixes 1–4, 6, 8, and 9.

There is a very rich literature on the experiences of the Japanese in California agriculture, the most important economic activity for members of the ethnic group on the mainland. Incidentally, a reading of this literature also will provide some important insights into the development of labor-intensive family farms and the role of ethnic ties in the development of what some scholars have called "ethnic enterprises." The classic piece on the contributions of the Japanese to California agriculture is that of Iwata (1962). The early years of Japanese involvement in California agriculture are described in Ichihashi's (1932) work. Useful source material on the conditions faced by Japanese farm laborers, including the reactions of white labor unions, is found in several U.S. government documents. These include U.S. Commissioner of Labor (1903), U.S. Department of Labor (1945), and U.S. Immigration Commission (1911). Modell (1977) analyzes the nature of Japanese involvement in intensive agriculture in the Los Angeles area before World War II. Hirabayashi and Tanaka (1988) describe the early development of the community with, after World War II, the largest single concentration of Japanese Americans on the mainland—Gardena, California. In the early 1900s Gardena was the center of strawberry production in Los Angeles County, a crop which the Issei dominated.

There has been considerable discussion among scholars about why the Japanese eventually came to occupy the small business niche, especially in agriculture. One view, best developed in Light (1972), emphasizes cultural factors, especially the use of tanomoshi or the rotating credit mechanism, which provided an alternative source of capital to start small businesses. Although his work has been criticized for overemphasizing the importance of the tanomoshi, it nonetheless should be read by all students interested in the relationship between ethnicity and business. A more "structural" approach suggesting that the Japanese were forced into the small business niche and emphasizing their middleman position is found in Modell (1977) and Bonacich and Modell (1980). "Ethnic hegemony," a somewhat different structural approach, has been proposed by Jiobu (1988) to account for Japanese American success in agriculture. An assessment of some of the different views of the relationship between ethnicity and the economic accommodation of the Japanese is found in O'Brien and Fugita (1982).

Several works dealing with the El Monte berry strike collectively provide insights into the complex relationships among the Japanese American ethnic community, Japanese and white farmers, Mexican laborers, and white officials. These include Hoffman (1973), Lopez (1970), Spaulding (1934), and Wollenberg (1972). Modell (1977) also includes some important historical details about the strike.

Recent oral histories of farm communities in California give the reader a feeling for what life was like in these isolated ethnic enclaves. See Masumoto (1987) for a description of Del Rey, Nakane (1985) for the Pajaro Valley, and Lukes and Okihiro (1985) for the Santa Clara Valley. In Ichioka's (1984) detailed article on the events leading up to and consequences of the Alien Land Law of 1920, he also discusses ways some of the Issei were able to skirt the law. Carrott (1983) analyzes the prejudicial decisions made by the Supreme Court against the Japanese in the 1920s.

A classic work dealing with the structure of the Japanese American community is Miyamoto's (1939) study of pre–World War II Seattle. The most anthropologically informed and insightful treatment of the transformations of Japanese American family and kin relationships through successive generations is found in the works of Yanagisako (1975; 1977; 1985). Other discussions of the family are found in Kitano and Kikumura (1980) and Suzuki (1980). Glenn (1981; 1986) examines the causes and consequences of doing domestic service work on three generational groups of Japanese American women. A discussion of the role played by the Buddhist Church in the development of the Japanese American community has been provided by Kashima (1977). A detailed description, informed by Japanese language sources, of Issei responses to early labor conditions is found in the numerous papers by Ichioka (e.g., 1971; 1977a; 1980). For the recollections of a key participant in many of these struggles see Yoneda (1983).

Finally, any effort to get a clearer perspective on Japanese American immigrant community life should include a comparison with other groups immigrating at about the same time. A good source in this regard is Handlin's (1951) seminal work on European immigration to the U.S.

2. PORTENTS OF THE INCARCERATION

Good historical discussions of the individuals and events involved in the decision to evacuate and incarcerate Japanese Americans are found in Daniels (1971; 1975) and Irons (1983). The latter highlights the struggles within the government and the four evacuation and incarceration cases that came before the Supreme Court. White (1979) provides some insights into Earl Warren's changing views of the incarceration and his actions relevant to it. The Commission on Wartime Relocation and Internment of Civilians (1982) details the findings of the Congressional committee that supported the redress proposal passed by both Houses of Congress and signed by President Reagan in 1988. Herzig (1984) defends the Commission's analysis that the Japanese diplomatic message code, MAGIC, neither implicated the loyalty of Japanese Americans nor played a major role in the decision to incarcerate them.

Papers by Culley (1984) and Ogawa (1978) deal with the question of why there was no mass evacuation and internment in Hawaii. Schwartz (in press) investigates the relationship between public opinion and public policy in the treatment of Japanese Americans during World War II. O'Neil (1981) compares American and Canadian policies and actions concerning their Japanese minorities during the war. Sundquist (1988) provides one of the most thoughtful and up-to-date discussions of the events surrounding the evacuation and incarceration.

3. THE CONCENTRATION CAMP EXPERIENCE

A historical and personalized description of both why and how Japanese Americans experienced the evacuation, internment, and incarceration is found in Weglyn (1976). This work includes vignettes that give the reader a sense of how ordinary people dealt with the sudden catastrophe and injustice in their lives. Other personal stories of Japanese Americans during this period are found in Tateishi (1984), Thomas (1952), and the Tule Lake Committee (1980). Spickard (1983) describes the transition of power within the Japanese community from the Issei to Nisei JACL members during the tumultuous 1941–1942 period. The official justification for the internment in 1942 as well as bureaucratic descriptions of details of the organization of camp life (including photographs) are found in a government document called *Final Report* (1978), recently reissued by a New York Times publishing outlet. Another official view of the events surrounding the incarceration is by the head of the WRA, Dillon Myer (1971). Recently, Drinnon (1987) has written critically about Myer's role. The War Relocation Authority's handling of Japanese American interests in their most important economic niche, farming, is described by Solberg and Eliot (1973).

The disruption of Japanese American family life, especially the breakdown of traditional authority and the demoralization of the older generation, is dealt with in a WRA report written by Spicer (1946). Broom and Kitsuse (1956) also deal with the impact of relocation, incarceration, and relocation on the family. A discussion of the relocation's disruption of Japanese American community is found in Saiki (1986). James (1987) points out some of the ironies involved in an educational system instituted behind barbed wire.

One of the most painful lingering effects of the internment for Japanese Americans is the turmoil caused by the infamous loyalty questions in 1943. Excellent ethnographic descriptions as well as commentaries on the trauma they caused are found in Christgau (1985), Spicer (1946), Thomas (1952), and Thomas and Nishimoto (1946).

A few books and articles describe the early post-incarceration adaptation of the internees. Thomas's (1952) second volume of the Japanese-American Evacuation and Resettlement Project discusses aspects of the 1943–44 resettlement to the Midwest and East. Sawada (1986–87) describes the dynamics of the development of one of the major eastern resettlement locations, Seabrook Farms in New Jersey. He focuses on the interplay between the labor needs of the farm and the WRA's need to relocate a large number of internees. A treatment of resettlement in Chicago and Nisei personality is found in Caudill and De Vos (1956).

In general, it has been very difficult to accurately assess the economic, social, and psychological consequences of the evacuation and internment. Relevant sources are Bloom and Reimer (1949), Broom and Kitsuse (1956), and the Commission on Wartime Relocation and Internment of Civilians (1982). The latter work was the basis for U.S. government action on redress. A recently published volume edited by Daniels, Taylor, and Kitano (1986) contains numerous papers on the various effects of the incarceration and the development of the redress movement.

4. POSTWAR ASSIMILATION

Because of significant differences in the experience of Hawaiian and West

Coast Japanese Americans, there are essentially two distinct bodies of literature dealing with the respective ethnic communities. Thus, for example, the literature on the post–World War II Hawaiian experience has devoted more attention to the emergence of Japanese in the political system, whereas the mainland literature has focused more on the issues surrounding the "model minority" controversy.

Survey-based studies such as those by Connor (1977), Levine and Rhodes (1981), and Montero (1980) provide evidence for the assimilation of Japanese Americans into the mainstream of American life. In part, these works show that succeeding generations of Japanese Americans are more and more likely to abandon elements of traditional Japanese culture and to adopt mainstream American cultural items. The major weakness of these works, however, is that they equate the abandonment of elements of traditional Japanese culture with the loss of ethnicity. An alternative view, presenting evidence of both assimilation and the persistence of ethnic community involvement among Japanese Americans, is found in Fugita and O'Brien (1991).

The educational and occupational characteristics of Japanese Americans following World War II are described in Kan and Liu (1986) and Nee and Wong (1985). The latter paper is important because it documents why the family is important for the economic and social success of an ethnic group. Papers which show that discrimination against Japanese Americans in the workplace still exists include Cabezas and Kawaguchi (1986) and Woodrum (1981). Hraba (1979) and others have raised the possibility that some of the income disparities between Japanese Americans (and other Asian Americans) and Caucasian Americans of comparable educational levels are due to Asian American interpersonal styles which are less effective in a white organizational context.

O'Brien and Fugita (1983a) present some data on how Japanese Americans view discrimination against themselves. The role of Japanese culture and the experience of growing up in a small business family on the eventual educational and occupational success of second and third generation Japanese Americans is examined in Fujimoto (1975) and O'Brien and Fugita (1982). A useful comparison of Japanese and American cultural values and their impact on Japanese Americans has been written by Yamamoto and Wagatsuma (1980), the first a Nisei, the second a native Japanese.

5. THE PERSISTENCE OF COMMUNITY

In order to put the question of ethnic community survival among Japanese Americans into proper perspective, it is necessary to have some understanding of ethnic community life among other immigrant ethnic groups. Reitz (1980) has provided a comparative framework for examining the persistence of several ethnic communities in Canada. A good treatment of American ethnic groups is found in Glazer and Moynihan's (1970) study of the transformation of various immigrant communities in New York

City. Some other helpful discussions of European immigrant groups in the United States include: Alba (1976), Alba and Chamlin (1983), Gordon (1964), Greeley (1974), Handlin (1951), and Yancey et al. (1985). A good comparison for Japanese American ethnic community life, particularly with regard to involvement in ethnic community associations is found in the research on Irish and Italian Americans reported by Goering (1971) and Roche (1982). The most comprehensive treatment of the current level of involvement of Japanese Americans in ethnic community life in a variety of urban and rural settings is found in Fugita and O'Brien (1977; 1985; 1991) and O'Brien and Fugita (1983b; 1984).

An insightful paper on Japanese American interpersonal style and how it helps to maintain ethnic community life is found in Miyamoto (1986–87). For an understanding of the roots of this style in Japanese culture as well as how it is manifested in that nation today, the reader can examine Dore (1986), Kidder (1987), Reischauer (1981), and Zander (1983). It should be emphasized that Japanese American interpersonal style is a product of both the culture which the immigrants brought with them from Japan and the adjustments individuals in the group have had to make in order to survive in the American situation.

Unfortunately, there is only a very small literature on the mental health consequences of having to deal with two very different kinds of interpersonal style. Two of the best available treatments of these issues are found in Lebra (1972) and Gehrie (1976). Lebra (1972) discusses the general differences in the interpersonal orientation of Japanese versus American culture. Gehrie (1976) describes some of the conflicts and difficulties experienced by third generation Sansei growing up in a white world.

The high level of involvement of Japanese Americans in voluntary associations today can be traced in large part to the historically important role of these types of organizations in facilitating the survival of the group, both in Japan and in the United States. For details on voluntary associations in Japan see Norbeck (1972). For details on voluntary associations among the Issei immigrant generation see Ichioka (1977a). A series of papers on the Nisei Farmers League (Fugita, 1978; Fugita and O'Brien 1977; O'Brien and Fugita 1984) relate the historical role of collective organization in Japanese American community life to its use in dealing with contemporary issues. These papers point out both the similarities and differences between the historical and contemporary roles of voluntary associations in this ethnic community.

6. THE FUTURE OF JAPANESE AMERICANS

Herbert Gans (1979) has written a useful paper drawing the distinction between interactional and symbolic ethnicity. Some other conceptually helpful discussions of ethnic change and persistence are Cohen (1981) and Yancey et al. (1976). Breton (1964) points out the importance of ethnic institutions in the persistence of community. Although it is much too soon to expect the full story on redress as a social movement to be written, some of its early aspects are discussed in Daniels, Taylor, and Kitano's (1986) edited volume. See especially the papers by Daniels, Tateishi, Hohri, and Minami.

For a discussion of the emergence, growth, and difficulties experienced by the Asian American Studies movement, see for example Murase (1976), Endo (1973), Endo and Wei (1988), and Trottier (1981). Francia (1983) articulates some of the issues involved in Asian American film making.

Kitano et al. (1984) have published the most recent intermarriage statistics on Japanese Americans along with other Asian Americans. A historical survey of Japanese American intermarriage has been conducted by Spickard 1980. For discussions of Japanese American organizational life and its relationship to ethnic group persistence see Levine and Rhodes (1981:78–81, 121–122), Oguri-Kendis (1979), and Fugita and O'Brien (1985).

REFERENCES

Agricultural Labor in California. 1940. Washington, D.C.: Government Printing Office.

Alba, Richard D. 1976. Social Assimilation among American Catholic National-Origin Groups. *American Sociological Review* 41:1030–1046.

Alba, Richard D. and Mitchell B. Chamlin. 1983. A Preliminary Examination of Ethnic Identification among Whites. *American Sociological Review* 48:240–247.

Albert, Michael D. 1980. Japanese American Communities in Chicago and the Twin Cities. Ph.D. dissertation, University of Minnesota. 318 pgs.

Arensberg, Conrad M. 1942. Report on a Developing Community, Poston, Arizona. *Applied Anthropology: Problems of Human Organization* 2:1–21.

Asian Week. 1989. 1/4 of Those Polled Think Asians Gaining Too Much. February 17, p.14.

Bailey, Thomas A. 1932. California, Japan, and the Alien Land Legislation of 1913. *Pacific Historical Review* 1:36–59.

Banfield, Edward C. and James Q. Wilson. 1963. *City Politics.* Cambridge, Mass.: Harvard University Press.

Beckman, Allan. 1989. A Nikkei Problem: Improper Identification. *Pacific Citizen.* 109 (20) December 22–29, E1, E16.

Beechert, Edward. 1977. Labor Relations in the Hawaiian Sugar Industry: 1850–1937. Paper presented at the Asian American Labor History Conference. University of California, Los Angeles, November 18.

Bellah, Robert N., Richard Madsen, William M. Sullivan, Ann Swidler, and Stephen M. Tipton. 1985. *Habits of the Heart: Individualism and Commitment in American Life.* Berkeley: University of California Press.

Benkin, Richard L. 1978. Ethnicity and Organization: Jewish Communities in Eastern Europe and the United States. *Sociological Quarterly* 19:614–625.

Bland, Richard, Brian Elliot, and Frank Bechhofer. 1978. Social Mobility in the Petite Bourgeoisie. *Acta sociologica* 21:229–248.

Bloom, Leonard and Ruth Riemer. 1949. *Removal and Return: The Socio-economic Effects of the War on Japanese Americans.* Berkeley: University of California Press.

Bonacich, Edna. 1973. A Theory of Middleman Minorities. *American Sociological Review* 38:583–594.

Bonacich, Edna, and John Modell. 1980. *The Economic Basis of Ethnic Solidarity: Small Business in the Japanese American Community.* Berkeley: University of California Press.

Bosworth, Allan. 1967. *America's Concentration Camps.* New York: Norton.

Breton, Raymond. 1964. Institutional Completeness of Ethnic Communi-

References

ties and the Personal Relations of Immigrants. *American Journal of Sociology* 70:193–205.

Brief of the Attorney General of California. 1922. *Records and Briefs.* 120, 123.

Broom, Leonard and John I. Kitsuse. 1956. *The Managed Casualty: The Japanese-American Family in World War II.* Berkeley: University of California Press.

Cabezas, Amado and Gary Kawaguchi. 1988. Empirical Evidence for Continuing Asian American Income Inequality: The Human Capital Model and Labor Market Segmentation. Pp. 144–164 in G. Y. Okihiro, S. Hune, A. A. Hansen, and J. M. Liu (eds.), *Reflections on Shattered Windows: Promises and Prospects for Asian American Studies.* Pullman: Washington State University Press.

Carrott, M. Browning. 1983. Prejudice Goes to Court: The Japanese and the Supreme Court in the 1920s. *California History* 63:126–138.

Castile, George P. 1981. Issues in the Analysis of Enduring Cultural Systems. Pp. xv–xxii in George Castile and Gilbert Kueshner (eds.), *Persistent People: Cultural Enclaves in Perspective.* Tucson: University of Arizona Press.

Caudill, William and George De Vos. 1956. Achievement, Culture and Personality: The Case of the Japanese Americans. *American Anthropologist* 58:1102–1126.

Chan, Sucheng. 1988. Asians in the United States: A Selected Bibliography of Writings Published since the 1960s. In G. Y. Okihiro, S. Hune, A. A. Hansen, and J. M. Liu (eds.), *Reflections on Shattered Windows: Promises and Prospects for Asian American Studies.* Pullman: Washington State University Press.

Cheng, Lucie. 1976. The Chinese American in Sociology. In E. Gee (ed.), *Counterpoint: Perspectives in Asian America.* Los Angeles: UCLA Asian American Studies Center.

Christgau, John. 1985. Collins versus the World: The Fight to Restore Citizenship to Japanese American Renunciants of World War II. *Pacific Historical Review* 54:1:1–31.

Chuman, Frank F. 1976. *The Bamboo People: The Law and Japanese Americans.* Del Mar, Calif.: Publishers Inc.

Cohen, Abner. 1981. Variables in Ethnicity. In C. F. Keyes (ed.), *Ethnic Change.* Seattle: University of Washington Press.

Commission on Wartime Relocation and Internment of Civilians. 1982. *Personal Justice Denied.* Washington, D.C.: Government Printing Office.

Connor, John W. 1974. Value Continuities and Change in Three Generations of Japanese Americans. *Ethos* 2: 232–264.

_____ . 1976. Joge Kankei: A Key Concept for an Understanding of Japanese-American Achievement. *Psychiatry* 39:266–279.

_____ . 1977. *Tradition and Change in Three Generations of Japanese Americans.* Chicago: Nelson-Hall.

References

Culley, John H. 1984. Relocation of Japanese Americans: The Hawaiian Experience. *Air Force Law Review* 24:176–183.

Daniels, Roger. 1966. Westerners from the East: Oriental Immigrants Reappraised. *Pacific Historical Review* 35:373–383.

———. 1971. *Concentration Camps USA: Japanese Americans and World War II*. New York: Holt, Rinehart & Winston.

———. 1974. *The Politics of Prejudice*. New York: Atheneum.

———. 1975. *The Decision to Relocate the Japanese Americans*. Philadelphia: J. B. Lippincott.

———. 1985. Japanese America, 1930–1941: An Ethnic Community in the Great Depression. *Journal of the West* 24:35–50.

———. 1986. The Redress Movement. In R. Daniels, S. C. Taylor, and H.H.L. Kitano (eds.), *Japanese Americans: From Relocation to Redress*. Salt Lake City: University of Utah Press.

———. 1988. *Asian America: Chinese and Japanese in the United States since 1950*. Seattle: University of Washington Press.

Daniels, Roger, Sandra C. Taylor, and Harry H. L. Kitano (eds.). 1986. *Japanese Americans: From Relocation to Redress*. Salt Lake City: University of Utah Press.

Dore, Ronald. 1986. *Flexible Rigidities: Industrial Policy and Structural Adjustment in the Japanese Economy 1970–80*. London: Athlone.

Drinnon, Richard. 1987. *Keeper of Concentration Camps: Dillion S. Meyer and American Racism*. Berkeley: University of California Press.

Durkheim, Emile. 1933. *The Division of Labor in Society*. New York: The Free Press.

Embree, John F. 1939. *Suya Mura: A Japanese Village*. Chicago: University of Chicago Press.

———. 1943. Resistance to Freedom—An Administrative Problem. *Applied Anthropology* 2:10–14.

Emi, Frank S. 1986. Draft Resistance at Heart Mountain. *Pacific Citizen*. December 19–26, Section A, pp. 58–61, 62.

Endo, Russell. 1973. Whither Ethnic Studies: A Reexamination of Some Issues. In S. Sue and N. N. Wagner (eds.), *Asian-Americans: Psychological Perspectives*. Ben Lomond, Calif.: Science and Behavior Books.

Endo, Russell, and William Wei. 1988. On the Development of Asian American Studies Programs. In G. Y. Okihiro, S. Hune, A. A. Hansen, and J. M. Liu (eds.), *Reflections on Shattered Windows: Promises and Prospects for Asian American Studies*. Pullman: Washington State University Press.

Ennis, Edward. 1981. Oral Testimony before the Commission on Wartime Relocation and Incarceration of Civilians. Washington, D.C.: November 2, p. 156.

Erickson, Kai. 1976. *Everything in Its Path*. New York: Simon & Schuster.

Fei, H. T. 1939. *Peasant Life in China: A Field Study of Country Life in the Yangtze Valley*. London: Routledge & Kegan Paul.

Final Report. 1978. *Final Report: Japanese Evacuation from the West Coast*,

References

1942. U.S. Department of War. New York: New York Times Arno Press.

Foner, Philip S. 1964. *History of the Labor Movement in the United States* (Vol. 3). New York: International.

Francia, Luis H. 1983. Made in America. *Film Comment* 19:56–58.

Freedman, M. 1964. The Family in China, Past and Present. In A. Feuerwerker (ed.), *Modern China*. Englewood Cliffs, N.J.: Prentice-Hall.

Fromm, Erich. 1941. *Escape from Freedom*. New York: Avon.

Fuchs, Lawrence H. 1961. *Hawaii Pono: A Social History*. New York: Harcourt, Brace & World.

Fugita, Stephen S. 1978. A Perceived Ethnic Factor in California's Farm Labor Conflict. *Explorations in Ethnic Studies* 1:50–72.

Fugita, Stephen S. and David J. O'Brien. 1977. Economics, Ideology and Ethnicity: The Struggle between the United Farm Workers Union and the Nisei Farmers League. *Social Problems* 25:146–156.

_____. 1985. Structural Assimilation, Ethnic Group Membership, and Political Participation among Japanese Americans: A Research Note. *Social Forces* 63:986–995.

_____. 1991. *Japanese Americans: The Persistence of Community*. Seattle: University of Washington Press.

Fugita, Stephen S., David J. O'Brien, and Sharon Kooney. 1984. Assimilation and Ethnic Community Involvement: Effects on Japanese American Divorce. Presented at the annual meetings of the Western Psychological Association. Los Angeles, April 5–8.

Fugita, Stephen S. and Henry T. Tanaka. 1987. The Japanese American Community in Cleveland. In D. D. Van Tassel (ed.), *Encyclopedia of Cleveland History*. Bloomington: Indiana University Press.

Fujimoto, Tetsuya. 1975. Social Class and Crime: The Case of the Japanese Americans. *Issues in Criminology* 10:86–87.

Fujita, Michinari. 1929. The Japanese Association in America. *Sociology and Social Research* 13: 211–228.

Gans, Herbert J. 1979. Symbolic Ethnicity: The Future of Ethnic Groups and Cultures in America. *Ethnic and Racial Studies* 2:1–20.

Gee, Emma (ed.). 1976. *Counterpoint: Perspectives on Asian America*. Los Angeles, Calif.: UCLA Asian American Studies Center.

Gehrie, Mark J. 1976. Childhood and Community: On the Experience of Japanese Americans in Chicago. *Ethos* 4:353–383.

Gendrot, Sophie and Joan Turner. 1983. Ethnicity and Class: Politics on Manhattan's Lower East Side. *Ethnic Groups* 5:79–108.

Girdner, Audrie and Anne Loftis. 1969. *The Great Betrayal*. New York: Macmillan.

Glazer, Nathan and Daniel P. Moynihan. 1970. *Beyond the Melting Pot: The Negroes, Puerto Ricans, Jews, Italians, and Irish of New York City*. Cambridge, Mass.: M.I.T. Press.

Glenn, Evelyn Nakano. 1981. Occupational Ghettoization: Japanese American Women and Domestic Service, 1905–1970. *Ethnicity* 8:352–386.

References

———. 1986. *Issei, Nisei, War Bride: Three Generations of Japanese American Women in Domestic Service.* Philadelphia: Temple University Press.

Goering, John M. 1971. The Emergence of Ethnic Interests: A Case of Serendipity. *Social Forces* 49:379–384.

Gordon, Milton. 1964. *Assimilation in American Life: The Role of Race, Religion, and National Origins.* New York: Oxford University Press.

Greeley, Andrew M. 1974. *Ethnicity in the United States: A Preliminary Reconnaisance.* New York: Wiley.

Haglund, Edna. 1984. Japan: Cultural Considerations. *International Journal of Intercultural Relations* 8:61–76.

Handlin, Oscar. 1951. *The Uprooted.* New York: Grosset & Dunlap.

Harrison, Laird. 1986. S.F. Cops Draft Plan to Report Anti-Asian Violence. *Asian Week* December 26. Pgs. 1, 19.

Hechter, Michael. 1975. *Internal Colonialism: The Celtic Fringe in British National Development, 1536–1966.* Berkeley: University of California Press.

Herzig, John A. 1984. Japanese Americans and MAGIC. *Amerasia Journal* 11:47–66.

Higgs, Robert. 1978. Landless by Law: Japanese Immigrants in California Agriculture to 1941. *Journal of Economic History* 38:205–225.

Hirabayashi, Lane R. and George Tanaka. 1988. The Issei Community in Moneta and the Gardena Valley, 1900–1920. *Southern California Quarterly* 70:127–158.

Hoffman, Abraham. 1973. The El Monte Berry Pickers Strike, 1933: International Involvement in a Local Labor Dispute. *Journal of the West* 12:71–84.

Hofstadter, Richard. 1955a. *The Age of Reform.* New York: Random House Vintage Books.

———. 1955b. *Social Darwinism in American Thought* (rev. ed.). Boston: Beacon Press.

Hohri, William. 1986. Redress as a Movement towards Enfranchisement. In R. Daniels, S. C. Taylor, and H.H.L. Kitano (eds.), *Japanese Americans: From Relocation to Redress.* Salt Lake City: University of Utah Press.

Honolulu Advertiser. 1942. February 28, 9:1.

Hosokawa, Bill. 1969. *Nisei: The Quiet Americans.* New York: Morrow.

Hraba, Joeseph. 1979. *American Ethnicity.* Itasca, Ill.: F. E. Peacock.

Hsu, Francis. 1971. Psychological Homeostasis and Jen: Concepts for Advancing Psychological Anthropology. *American Anthropologist* 73:23–41.

———. 1975. *Iemoto: The Heart of Japan.* Cambridge, Mass.: Schenkman.

———. 1983. *Rugged Individualism Reconsidered: Essays in Psychological Anthropology.* Knoxville: University of Tennessee Press.

Hurh, Won Moo and Kwang Chung Kim. 1986. Success Image of Asian Americans: Its Validity, Practical and Theoretical Implications. Presented at the annual meetings of the American Sociological Association, New York, August 30-September 3.

References

Ichihashi, Yamato. 1932. *Japanese in the United States*. Stanford: Stanford University Press.

Ichioka, Yuji. 1971. A Buried Past: Early Issei Socialists and the Japanese Community. *Amerasia* 1:25–37.

_____. 1976. A Buried Past: A Survey of English-Language Works of Japanese American History. In Emma Gee (ed.). *Counterpoint: Perspectives on Asian America*. Los Angeles: Asian American Studies Center, UCLA.

_____. 1977a. Japanese Associations and the Japanese Government: A Special Relationship 1909–1926. *Pacific Historical Review* 46:409–438.

_____. 1977b. The Early Japanese Immmigrant Quest for Citizenship: The Background of the 1922 Ozawa Case. *Amerasia* 4:1–22.

_____. 1980. Japanese Labor Contractors and the Northern Pacific and the Great Northern Railroad Companies, 1898–1907. *Labor History* 21:325–350.

_____. 1984. Japanese Immigrant Response to the 1920 California Alien Land Law. *Agricultural History* 36:157–178.

_____. 1988. *The Issei: The World of the First Generation Japanese Immigrants, 1885–1924*. New York: Free Press.

Ike, Nobutaka. 1947. Taxation and Land Ownership in the Westernization of Japan. *Journal of Economic History* 7:160–182.

Irons, Peter. 1983. *Justice at War*. New York: Oxford University Press.

Ito, Kazuo. 1973. *Issei: A History of Japanese Immigrants in North America*. Seattle: Executive Committee for Publication of Issei: A History of Japanese Immigrants in North America.

Iwata, Edward. 1988. For Asians, "Great Wall" Must Break. *Los Angeles Times*, September 2.

Iwata, Masakazu. 1962. The Japanese Immigrants in California Agriculture. *Agricultural History* 36:25–37.

James, Thomas. 1987. *Exile Within: The Schooling of Japanese Americans 1942–1945*. Cambridge, Mass.: Harvard University Press.

Jiobu, Robert W. 1988. *Ethnicity and Assimilation*. Albany: State University of New York Press.

Johnson, C. 1962. *Peasant Nationalism and Community Power: The Emergence of Revolutionary China*. Stanford, Calif.: Stanford University Press.

Johnson, Colleen L. 1976. The Principle of Generation among the Japanese in Honolulu. *Ethnic Groups* 1:18–35.

Kan, Stephen H. and William T. Liu. 1986. The Educational Status of Asian Americans: An Update from the 1980 Census. In Nobuyu Tsuchida (ed.), *Issues in Asian and Pacific American Education*. Minneapolis: Asian/Pacific American Learning Resource Center.

Kashima, Tetsuden. 1977. *Buddhism in America: The Social Organization of an Ethnic Religious Institution*. Westport, Conn.: Greenwood Press.

Kidder, Louise H. 1987. There Is No Word for "Fair"—Notes from Japan. *Internationally Speaking*, 12: 1, 30–35.

Kim, Kwang C., Won M. Hurh, and Marilyn Fernandez. 1988. Intragroup

Differences in Business Participation: Three Asian Immigrant Groups. *International Migration Review* 23:73–95.

Kitano, Harry H. L. 1976. *Japanese Americans: The Evolution of a Subculture* (2nd ed.). Englewood Cliffs, N.J.: Prentice-Hall.

Kitano, Harry H. L. and Akemi Kikumura. 1980. The Japanese American Family. In R. Endo, S. Sue, and N. N. Wagner (eds.), *Asian Americans: Social and Psychological Perspectives*, Vol. II. Ben Lomond, Calif.: Science and Behavior Books.

Kitano, Harry H. L., Wai-Tsang Yeung, Lynn Chai, and Herbert Hatanaka. 1984. Asian American Interracial Marriage. *Journal of Marriage and the Family* 46:179–190.

Kotani, Roland. 1985. *The Japanese in Hawaii: A Century of Struggle*. Honolulu: Hawaii Hochi, Ltd.

Lasch, Christopher. 1979. *The Culture of Narcissism: American Life in an Age of Diminishing Expectations*. New York: W. W. Norton Warner Books.

Lebra, Takie S. 1972. Acculturation Dilemma: The Function of Japanese Moral Values for Americanization. *Council on Anthropology and Education Newsletter*, 3:6–13.

Levine, Gene N. and Colbert Rhodes. 1981. *The Japanese American Community: A Three Generation Study*. New York: Praeger.

Light, Ivan. 1972. *Ethnic Enterprise in America*. Berkeley: University of California Press.

Lopez, Ronald W. 1970. The El Monte Berry Strike of 1933. *Atzlan* I:101–114.

Lukes, Timothy J. and Gary Y. Okihiro. 1985. *Japanese Legacy: Farming and Community Life in California's Santa Clara Valley*. Cupertino, Calif.: California History Center.

Lyman, Stanford M. 1977. Generation and Character: The Case of the Japanese Americans. Pp. 151–176 in S. Lyman (ed.), *The Asian in North America*. Santa Barbara, Calif.: ABC.

Lyons, Judith A. 1989. U.S. Civil Rights Panel Plans Investigation of "Glass Ceiling." *Asian Week*. 10:1,16.

McWilliams, Carey. 1944. *Prejudice; Japanese Americans: Symbols of Intolerance*. Boston: Little, Brown.

Massey, Douglas S. and Nancy A. Denton. 1988. Suburbanization and Segregation in U.S. Metropolitan Areas. *American Journal of Sociology* 94:592–626.

Masumoto, David M. 1987. *Country Voices: The Oral History of a Japanese American Family Farm Community*. Del Rey, Calif.: Inaka Countryside Publications.

Maykovich, Minako. 1971. White-Yellow Stereotypes: An Empirical Study. *Pacific Sociological Review* 14: 447–467.

Melloan, George. 1988. An American Views Japan's Copycat Culture. *Wall Street Journal*. July 12. Pg. 29.

Millis, H. A. 1915. Some of the Economic Aspects of Japanese Immigration. *American Economic Review* 5:787–804.

Minami, Dale. 1986. Coram nobis and Redress. In R. Daniels, S. C. Taylor,

References

and H.H.L. Kitano (eds.), *Japanese Americans: From Relocation to Redress*. Salt Lake City: University of Utah Press.

Miyakawa, T. Scott. 1974. Review of Daniels's *The Politics of Prejudice*. *Southern California Quarterly*:107–108.

Miyamoto, S. Frank. 1939. *Social Solidarity among the Japanese of Seattle*. Seattle: University of Washington, Publications in the Social Sciences, vol. II, no. 2.

_____. 1986–87. Problems of Interpersonal Style among the Nisei. *Amerasia* 13:29–45.

Modell, John. 1969. Class or Ethnic Solidarity: The Japanese American Union. *Pacific Historical Review* 38:193–206.

_____. 1977. *The Economics and Politics of Racial Accomodation: The Japanese of Los Angeles 1900–1942*. Urbana: University of Illinois Press.

Montero, Darrel. 1980. *Japanese Americans: Changing Patterns of Ethnic Affiliation over Three Generations*. Boulder, Colo.: Westview Press.

Moriyama, Alan T. 1984. The Causes of Emigration: The Background of Japanese Emigration to Hawaii, 1885–1894. In L. Cheng and E. Bonacich (eds.), *Labor Immigration under Capitalism*. Berkeley: University of California Press.

_____. 1985. *Imingaisha: Japanese Emigration Companies and Hawaii, 1894–1908*. Honolulu: University of Hawaii Press.

Munson, Curtis B. 1942. Report on Hawaiian Islands. In *Pearl Harbor Attack*, Hearings before the Joint Committee on the Investigation of the Pearl Harbor Attack, 79th Congress, 1st Session, pt. 6, pp. 2692–2696.

Murase, Mike. 1976. Ethnic Studies and Higher Education for Asian Americans. In E. Gee (ed.), *Counterpoint: Perspectives on Asian America*. Los Angeles: UCLA Asian American Studies Center.

Myer, Dillon S. 1971. *Uprooted Americans: The Japanese Americans and the War Relocation Authority during World War II*. Tucson: University of Arizona Press.

Nakane, Chie. 1970. *Japanese Society*. Berkeley: University of California Press.

Nakane, Kazuko. 1985. *Nothing Left in My Hands: An Early Japanese American Community in California's Pajaro Valley*. Seattle: Young Pine Press.

Nakatsu, Dan. 1988. America's Secret Weapon of World War II. pp. 76–84 in T. Ichinokuchi (ed.), *John Aiso and the M.I.S.: Japanese-American Soldiers in the Military Intelligence Service in World War II*. Los Angeles: Military Intelligence Service Club of Southern California.

Nee, Victor and Herbert Y. Wong. 1985. Asian American Socioeconomic Achievement: The Strength of the Family Bond. *Sociological Perspectives* 28:281–306.

Ng, Wendy L. 1989. Knowing the Past: Collective Memory and the Japanese American Experience. Paper presented at the annual meeting of the Association for Asian American Studies, New York, June 1–3.

Nisbet, Robert A. 1962. *Community and Power*. New York: Oxford University Press. (First published in 1953 under the title *Quest for Community*).

162

Norbeck, Edward. 1972. Japanese Common-Interest Associations in Cross-Cultural Perspective. *Journal of Voluntary Action Research* 1:38–41.

Novak, Michael. 1972. *The Rise of the Unmeltable Ethnics.* New York: Macmillan.

O'Brien, David J. 1975. *Neighborhood Organization and Interest-Group Processes.* Princeton, N.J.: Princeton University Press.

O'Brien, David J. and Stephen S. Fugita. 1982. Middleman Minority Concept: Its Explanatory Value in the Case of the Japanese in California Agriculture. *Pacific Sociological Review* 25:185–204.

_____. 1983a. Generational Differences in Japanese Americans' Perceptions and Feelings about Social Relationships between Themselves and Caucasian Americans. Pp. 223–240 in W. C. McCready (ed.), *Culture, Ethnicity, and Identity: Current Issues in Research.* New York: Academic Press.

_____. 1983b. Ethnic Population Size and the Maintenance of Ethnic Community Life: A Re-examination of the Subcultural Theory of Urbanism. Presented at the annual meetings of the Rural Sociological Society. Lexington, Kentucky, August 17–20.

_____. 1984. The Mobilization of a Traditionally Petit Bourgeois Ethnic Group. *Social forces* 63:522–537.

Ogawa, Dennis M. 1978. *Kodomo No Tami Ni (For the Sake of the Children): The Japanese American Experience in Hawaii.* Honolulu: University of Hawaii Press.

Ogura, Kosei. 1932. A Sociological Study of the Buddhist Churches of North America. Master's thesis. Los Angeles, Calif.: University of Southern California.

Oguri-Kendis, Kaoru. 1979. Ethnicity in the Suburbs: The Case of the Third Generation Japanese American. Paper presented at the annual meeting of the American Anthropological Association. Cincinnati, December 1.

Okihiro, Gary Y. 1984. Religion and Resistance in America's Concentration Camps. *Phylon* 45:220–233.

Okihiro, Gary Y., Shirley Hune, Arthur A. Hansen, and John M. Liu (eds.). 1988. *Reflections on Shattered Windows.* Pullman: Washington State University Press.

Olson, Mancur. 1971. *The Logic of Collective Action.* Cambridge, Mass.: Harvard University Press.

O'Neil, Daniel J. 1981. American vs. Canadian Policies toward Their Japanese Minorities during the Second World War. *Comparative Social Research* 4:111–134.

Oren, Dan A. 1985. *Joining the Club: A History of Jews and Yale.* New Haven: Yale University Press.

Osajima, Keith H. 1988. Asian Americans as the Model Minority: An Analysis of the Popular Press Image in the 1960s and 1980s. In G. Y. Okihiro, S. Hune, A. A. Hansen, and J. M. Liu (eds.), *Reflections on Shattered Windows: Promises and Prospects for Asian American Studies.* Pullman, Wash.: Washington State University Press.

References

_____. 1989. Internalized Racism and the Educational Experience of Asian American College Students. Paper presented at the annual meeting of the Association for Asian American Studies, New York: June 1–3.

Ouchi, William. 1984. *The M-Form Society: How American Teamwork Can Recapture the Competitive Edge*. Reading, Mass.: Addison-Wesley.

Peterson, William. 1970. Success Story, Japanese American Style. Pp. 169–178 in Minako Kurokawa (ed.), *Minority Responses*. New York: Random House.

Reischauer, Edwin O. 1981. *The Japanese*. Cambridge, Mass.: Belknap Press of Harvard University Press.

Reitz, Jeffrey G. 1980. *The Survival of Ethnic Groups*. Toronto: McGraw-Hill Ryerson.

Roche, John P. 1982. Suburban Ethnicity: Ethnic Attitudes and Behavior among Italian Americans in Two Suburban Communities. *Social Science Quarterly* 63:145–153.

Rogers, Terence, and Satoru Izutsu. 1980. The Japanese. In J. F. McDermott, W. S. Tseng, and T. M. Maretzki (eds.), *Peoples and Cultures in Hawaii: A Psychocultural Profile*. Honolulu: University of Hawaii Press.

Saiki, Barry. 1986. The Uprooting of My Two Communities. In R. Daniels, S. C. Taylor, and H.H.L. Kitano (eds.) *Japanese Americans: From Relocation to Redress*. Salt Lake City: University of Utah Press.

Sawada, Mitziko. 1986–87. After the Camps: Seabrook Farms, New Jersey, and the Resettlement of Japanese Americans, 1944–47. *Amerasia Journal* 13:117–136.

Saxton, Alexander. 1971. *The Indispensable Enemy: Labor and the Anti-Chinese Movement in California*. Berkeley: University of California Press.

Schwartz, John. 1987. A "Superminority" Tops Out; Asian-Americans Confront Job Discrimination—and Struggle to Fit In. *Newsweek* 109:48.

Schwartz, Mildred A. In press. Public Opinion and Public Policy: Treatment of Japanese Residents in World War II. In M. Lubis (ed.), *Public Policy, Canada and the United States*. Westport, Conn.: Greenwood Press.

Shimo, Cedric. 1986. The Nisei of the 1800 Engineer Battalion: An Untold Story. *Pacific Citizen*. December 19–26, Section B, pp. 39–40, 52.

Solberg, C. Edward and Stephen M. Eliot. 1973. The War Relocation Authority and the Future of Japanese American Agriculture: A Continuing Study. Presented at the annual meeting of the Western Conference of the Association for Asian Studies, September 28–30.

Spaulding, Charles B. 1934. The Mexican Strike at El Monte, California. *Sociology and Social Research* 58:571–580.

Spicer, Edward H. 1946. *Impounded People: Japanese Americans in the Relocation Centers*. War Relocation Authority, U.S. Government Printing Office.

Spickard, Paul R. 1980. Japanese Americans and Intermarriage: A Historical Survey. Paper presented at the annual meeting of the Association for Asian and Pacific American Studies.

_____ . 1983. The Nisei Assume Power: The Japanese American Citizen's League, 1941–42. *Pacific Historical Review* 52:147–174.

_____ . 1989. *Mixed Blood: Intermarriage in Twentieth Century America.* Madison: University of Wisconsin Press.

Sumiya, Mikio. 1963. *Social Impact of Industrialization in Japan.* New York: Japanese National Commission for UNESCO.

Sundquist, Eric J. 1988. The Japanese-American Internment: A Reappraisal. *American Scholar* 57:529–547.

Suomisto, Laurel. 1988. Nisei Point to Ancient Barriers. *Daily Breeze* December 16. Pages 1, 20.

Suzuki, Bob H. 1980. The Asian American Family. In M. Fantini and R. Cardenas (eds.), *Parenting in a Multicultural Society.* New York: Longman.

Synnott, Marcia G. 1979. *The Half Opened Door: Discrimination and Admissions at Harvard, Yale, and Princeton, 1900–1970.* Westport, Conn.: Greenwood Press.

Tachiki, Amy, Eddie Wong, and Franklin Odo (eds.). 1971. *Roots: An Asian American Reader.* Los Angeles, Calif.: UCLA Asian American Studies Center.

Tateishi, John. 1984. *And Justice for All: An Oral History of the Japanese American Detention Camps.* New York: Random House.

_____ . 1986. The Japanese American Citizens League and the Struggle for Redress. In R. Daniels, S. C. Taylor, and Harry H. L. Kitano (eds.), *Japanese Americans: From Relocation to Redress.* Salt Lake City: University of Utah Press.

Taylor, Sandra C. 1986. Evacuation and Economic Loss: Questions and Perspectives. Pp. 163–167 in R. Daniels, S. C. Taylor, and H.H.L. Kitano (eds.) *Japanese Americans: From Relocation to Redress.* Salt Lake City: University of Utah.

Thomas, Dorothy S. 1952. *The Salvage.* Berkeley: University of California Press.

Thomas, Dorothy S. and Richard Nishimoto. 1946. *The Spoilage.* Berkeley: University of California Press.

Thomas, W. I. and Florian Znaniecki. 1927. *The Polish Peasant in Europe and America.* New York: Alfred A. Knopf.

Torres, Vicki. 1988. U.S.: Open Arms, Closed Minds. *Daily Breeze.* December 15. Pages A1, A12.

Trottier, Richard W. 1981. Charters of Panethnic Identity: Indigenous American Indians and Immigrant Asian Americans. In C. F. Keyes (ed.), *Ethnic Change.* Seattle: University of Washington Press.

Tsai, Shih-shan H. 1986. *The Chinese Experience in America.* Bloomington: Indiana University Press.

Tsuang, Grace W. 1989. Assuring Equal Access of Asian Americans to Highly Selective Universities. *Yale Law Journal* 98:659–678.

Tsuchida, Nobuya. 1978. By Choice or by Circumstance? Japanese Gardeners in Southern California, 1900–1941. Presented at the Asian American Labor History Conference. University of California, Los Angeles, February 10.

References

Tule Lake Committee. 1980. *Kinenhi: Reflections on Tule Lake*. San Francisco.

U.S. Bureau of the Census. 1872. *Ninth Census of the United States, 1870: A Compendium*. Washington, D.C.: U.S. Census Office.

———. 1904. *Twelfth Census of the United States. Taken in the Year 1900. Population. Special Reports. Occupations*. Washington, D.C.: U.S. Census Office.

———. 1923. *Fourteenth Census of the United States. Taken in the Year 1920. Volume IV. Population. Special Reports. Occupations*. Washington, D.C.: U.S. Bureau of the Census.

———. 1933. *Fifteenth Census of the United States: 1930. Population. Volume V. General Report on Occupations*. Washington, D.C.: U.S. Bureau of the Census.

———. 1943. *Sixteenth Census of the United States: 1940. Population. Subject Reports. Characteristics of the Nonwhite Population by Race*. Washington, D.C.: U.S. Bureau of the Census.

———. 1953. *Seventeenth Census of the United States: 1950. Population. Subject Reports. Characteristics of the Nonwhite Population by Race*. Washington, D.C.: U.S. Bureau of the Census.

———. 1963. *U.S. Census of Population: 1960. Subject Reports. Characteristics of the Nonwhite Population by Race*. Washington, D.C.: U.S. Bureau of the Census.

———. 1973. *1970 Census of the Population. Subject Reports. Japanese, Chinese, and Filipinos in the United States*. Washington, D.C.: U.S. Bureau of the Census.

———. 1975. *Historical Statistics of the United States: Colonial Times to 1970. Part 1*. Washington, D.C.: U.S. Bureau of the Census.

———. 1983a. *1980 Census of the Population. Ancestry of the Population by State: 1980. Supplementary Report. PC80-S1–10*. Washington, D.C.: U.S. Bureau of the Census.

———. 1983b. *1980 Census of the Population. Volume 1, Charatteristics of the Population, Chapter B, General Population Characteristics, Part 1, United States Summary. PC80–1-B1*. Washington, D.C.: U.S. Bureau of the Census.

———. 1983c. *1980 Census of the Population. Volume 1, Characteristics of the Population, Chapter C, General Social and Economic Characteristics, Part 1, United States Summary. PC80–1-C1*. Washington, D.C.: U.S. Bureau of the Census.

———. 1988. *Statistical Abstract of the United States: 1988*. Washington, D.C.: U.S. Bureau of the Census.

U.S. Commissioner of Labor. 1903. *Second Report of the Commissioner of Labor on Hawaii, 1902*. Washington, D.C.: Government Printing Office.

U.S. Congress Select Committee. 1942. U.S. Congress, House, Select Committee Investigating National Defense Migration. *Hearings* 77th Congress 2nd Session (Washington, D.C.).

U.S. Department of Labor. 1945. *Labor Unionism in American Agriculture*. Washington, D.C.: Government Printing Office.

U.S. Immigration Commission. 1911. *Immigrants in Industries, Part 25:*

References

Japanese and Other Immigrant Races in the Pacific Coast and Rocky Mountain States. Washington, D.C.: U.S. Government Printing Office.

Weglyn, Michi. 1976. *Years of Infamy: The Untold Story of America's Concentration Camps.* New York: William Morrow.

Weisz, John R., Fred R. Rothbaum, Thomas C. Blackburn. 1984. Standing Out and Standing In: The Psychology of Control in America and Japan. *American Psychologist* 3:955–969.

White, G. Edward. 1979. The Unacknowledged Lesson: Earl Warren and the Japanese Relocation Controversy. *Virginia Quarterly Review* 55:613–29.

Whyte, William F. 1981. *Street Corner Society: The Social Structure of an Italian Slum* (3rd ed.). Chicago: University of Chicago Press.

Wiley, Norbert F. 1967. The Ethnic Mobility Trap and Stratification Theory. *Social Problems* 15:147–159.

Wilson, Robert A. and Bill Hosokawa. 1980. *East to America: A History of the Japanese in the United States.* New York: William Morrow.

Wollenberg, Charles. 1972. Race and Class in Rural California: The El Monte Berry Strike of 1933. *California Historical Quarterly* 2:155–164.

Woodrum, Eric. 1981. An Assessment of Japanese American Assimilation, Pluralism, and Subordination. *American Journal of Sociology* 87:157–169.

Yamamoto, George. 1959. Political Participation among Orientals in Hawaii. *Sociology and Social Research* 43:360.

Yamamoto, Joe and Wagatsuma, Hiroshi. 1980. The Japanese and Japanese Americans. *Journal of Operational Psychiatry* 11:120–135.

Yanagisako, Sylvia J. 1975. Two Processes of Change in Japanese-American Kinship. *Journal of Anthropological Research* 31:196–224.

———. 1977. Women-Centered Kin Networks in Urban Bilateral Kinship. *American Ethnologist* 4:207–266.

———. 1985. *Transforming the Past: Tradition and Kinship among Japanese Americans.* Stanford, Calif.: Stanford University Press.

Yancey, William L., Eugene P. Ericksen, and Richard N. Juliani. 1976. Emergent Ethnicity: A Review and Reformulation. *American Sociological Review* 41:391–402.

Yancey, William L., Eugene P. Erickson, and George H. Leon. 1985. The Structure of Pluralism: We're All Italian around Here, Aren't We, Mrs. O'Brien? *Ethnic and Racial Studies* 8:94–116.

Yano, Kiyoshi. 1988. Participating in the Mainstream of American Life amidst the Drawback of Racial Prejudice and Discrimination. Pp. 4–35 in T. Ichinokuchi (ed.), *John Aiso and the M.I.S.: Japanese-American Soldiers in the Military Intelligence Service, World War II.* Los Angeles: Military Intelligence Service Club of Southern California.

Yatsuhiro, Toshio, Iwao Ishino, and Yoshiharu Matsumoto. 1944. The Japanese-American Looks at Resettlement. *Public Opinion Quarterly* 8:188–201.

Yoder, Fred R. 1936. The Japanese Rural Community. *Rural Sociology* 1:420–429.

References

Yoneda, Karl. 1967. *History of Japanese Laborers in the U.S.* Tokyo: Shin Nihon Shuppon-Sha.

_____ . *Ganbatte: Sixty-Year Struggle of a Kibei Worker.* Los Angeles: UCLA Asian American Studies Center.

Zander, Alvin. 1983. The Value of Belonging to a Group in Japan. *Small Group Behavior* 14:3–14.

Zinsmeister, Karl. 1987. Prejudice against Asians: Anxiety and Acceptance. *Current* 297:37–40.

INDEX

Acculturation, defined, 83. See also Assimilation
ACLU, 47, 49, 68
Affirmative action, 131
AFL, 20–21. See also Labor unions
African Americans: in California, 119; Japanese Americans compared to, 35; and Japanese American small business owners, 129–30; number of, 137; segregation of, 35, 83–84
Agricultural workers. See Farm workers
Aiso, John, 65
Alien land acts: in Arizona, 27; in California, 22–26; effects of, 24–26, 27, 30–31, 149; in Idaho, 27; and Japanese American farm workers, 22–27; and Japanese American voluntary associations, 113; in Kansas, 27; in Louisiana, 27; in Montana, 27; in Nebraska, 27; in New Mexico, 27; in Oregon, 27; purposes of, 12–13; reactions to, 39; in Texas, 27; in Washington, 27. See also Discrimination against Japanese Americans
Amerasia Bookstore in Little Tokyo, 147
Amerasia Journal, 147
American Civil Liberties Union (ACLU), 47, 49, 68
American Federation of Labor (AFL), 20–21. See also Labor unions
Antimiscegenation laws, 98. See also Discrimination against Japanese Americans; Intermarriage of Japanese Americans
"Application for Leave Clearance," 69–72
Arizona, alien land acts in, 27
Armed forces. See Military forces
Armenian Americans, 122
Army. See Military forces
Arranged marriages of Japanese Americans, 99
Ascriptive ties, defined, 28
Asian American studies programs, 122–24, 147

Assimilation of European Americans, 83–84, 93–94, 101–2
Assimilation of Japanese Americans: in California, 119–20; causes of, 84–100; characteristics of, 1–2; and collective organization, 85; and community, 85; effects of, 133–34, 152; and ethnic economy, 85; and family structure, 85, 97; of Nisei, 91–92; and political power, 132; and relativistic ethic, 9–10, 85; of small business owners, 85, 92–93; and War Relocation Authority, 75, 85, 91, 92
Assimilation of Jewish Americans, 112

Bakke case, 131
Battle of Midway, 65
"Bearing up," 78
Bernstein, Joan Z., 81
Blacks. See African Americans
Bowling leagues of Japanese Americans, 102
Brooke, Edward W., 81
Bryan, William Jennings, 23–24
"Buddhaheads," 36
Buddhist Churches of America, 50. See also Buddhist temples
Buddhist priests, 64
Buddhist temples, 34, 36, 50, 63–64
Burns, John, 87
Business and professional groups of Japanese Americans, 34, 36, 102, 115

California, African Americans in, 119
California, Japanese Americans in: and alien land acts, 22–26; assimilation of, 119–20; discrimination against, 88, 98, 129; education of, 88–89; and ethnic economy, 89, 95–96; as farm workers, 19–27, 29, 39, 146; in labor unions, 20, 21; number of, 35; segregation of, 88. See also West Coast, Japanese Americans on
Camp Savage, Minnesota, 65, 68
Cannery and Agricultural Workers

169

Index

Union (CAWU), 30. See also Labor unions

Caucasians. See White Americans

CAWU, 30. See also Labor unions

Central California Contractors Association, 20. See also Labor unions

Central Japanese Association of Southern California, 30, 31. See also Japanese Associations

Chin, Vincent, 104

Chinda (Japanese ambassador), 23

Chinese Americans: in domestic service, 18; on East Coast, 18, 138; education of, 94, 144; family structure of, 33; as farm workers, 18, 21, 22; and Gold Rush, 17; income of, 144; Japanese Americans compared to, 16–18, 19; in manufacturing jobs, 18; in mechanical occupations, 18; in Midwest, 138; number of, 17, 137; in personal service, 18; reactions to, 17; in South, 138; time of immigration of, 17, 137; and transcontinental railroad, 17; urbanization of, 18; on West Coast, 18, 119–20, 138

Chinese Exclusion Act (1882), 17

Citizenship of European Americans, 39

Citizenship of Japanese Americans, 73–74, 87

Civic clubs of Japanese Americans, 115

Civil Liberties Act (1988), 67, 81

Clark, Mark, 45

Cold War, 90–91

Collective organization of Japanese Americans: and assimilation, 85; of community, 34, 113; of cooperatives, 27; and education, 96; and employment, 96; and ethnic economy, 133; and ethnicity, 6, 7, 8, 19, 147; and evacuation and internment, 42, 78–79, 133; of family structure, 117; of farm workers, 19, 27, 39, 95; importance of, 135; individualism compared to, 105–6, 108, 115–16; of Issei, 3, 5–6, 70, 91; of Japanese American Citizens League, 42; of Nisei, 36–37; origins of, 133; of partnerships, 27; and relativistic ethic, 8, 9, 36, 93, 94, 116–17, 133; of small business owners, 38, 93; and voluntary associations, 113, 133, 153. See also Interpersonal relationships of Japanese Americans

Colleges and universities, Japanese Americans in, 130–31

Colleges and universities, Jewish Americans in, 130, 131

Collins, Wayne, 73–74

Commission on Wartime Relocation and Internment of Civilians, 74, 81, 150

Communist party, 47–48

Community of Japanese Americans: and assimilation, 85; collective organization of, 34, 113; homogeneity of, 33; and Japanese government, 34; preservation of, 114; types of, 34

Concentration camps. See Evacuation and internment of Japanese Americans

Conscription law in Japan, 11

Constitution, Japanese, 4

Contract laborers, Japanese American, 12, 16, 19, 20. See also Farm workers, Japanese American

Conversion of Japanese Americans, 64

Cooperatives of Japanese Americans, 27, 29

Credit associations of Japanese Americans, 27–28, 149

Cultural assimilation, defined, 83. See also Assimilation

Cultural diversity in United States, 41

Cultural groups of Japanese Americans, 102

Cultural relativism. See Relativistic ethic of Japanese Americans

CWRIC, 81, 150

Daily Pinion (student newspaper), 50

Defense plants, Japanese Americans in, 64

Dekasegi rodo, defined, 11

Del E. Webb Company, 62

Democratic party, 87

Deportation of Japanese Americans, 73–74

Depression, 38, 91

De Witt, John L., 45–46, 48, 60, 65

Dingell, John, 127

Discrimination against Japanese Americans: in California, 88, 98, 129; against farm workers, 38; and Japanese American Citizens League, 113–14; against Nisei, 39, 103; and political power, 135; against Sansei, 103, 104; against small business owners, 38; types of, 103–4; and voluntary associations, 134–35. See also Alien land acts; Antimiscegenation laws; Evacuation and internment of Japanese Americans; Hate crimes; Reverse discrimination; Segregation of Japanese Americans; Terrorism against Japanese Americans; Toyota bashing parties

Domestic service, Chinese Americans in, 18

Draft resistance movement of Japanese Americans, 67–68, 82

Drinan, Robert, 81

East Coast, Chinese Americans on, 18, 138

East Coast, Japanese Americans on, 18, 91, 138

East Coast, white Americans on, 138

Education of Chinese Americans, 94, 144

Education of Japanese Americans: amount of, 90, 94, 144; in California, 88–89; and collective organization, 96; at colleges and universities, 130–31; and employment, 104; of farm workers, 19; of Issei, 94; and Meiji Restoration, 94; of Nisei, 38–39

Education of white Americans, 144

1800 Engineer Service Battalion, 68. See also Military forces

El Monte berry strike, 30–31

Emigration Protection Ordinance (1894), 12

Employment in United States, percentage distribution of, 143

Employment of Chinese Americans, 142. See also specific careers

Employment of Japanese Americans, 1, 96, 104, 141. See also specific careers

Enemy Alien Control Unit, 68

Entrepreneurial ideology, defined, 92–93. See also Small business owners, Japanese American

Estate of Tesubumi Yano case, 25

Ethnic economy of Japanese Americans: and assimilation, 85; in California, 89, 95–96; characteristics of, 29, 89; and collective organization, 133; and co-operatives, 29; defined, 6; and farm workers, 29; and Issei, 6; origins of, 8, 28, 38, 148; and small business owners, 28–29

Ethnic hegemony of Japanese Americans, 95, 149

Ethnicity of European Americans, 5, 33, 121, 122

Ethnicity of Japanese Americans: and collective organization, 6, 7, 8, 19, 147; and feudalism, 6–8; and homogeneity, 3–5, 33; and iemoto, 7; and intermarriage, 99, 125; and redress movement, 121, 124; and relativistic ethic, 8–10; and sojourner mentality, 11; symbolic aspects of, 120–21, 124, 125

Ethnic organizations of Japanese Americans. See Bowling leagues of Japanese Americans; Business and professional groups of Japanese Americans; Cultural groups of Japanese Americans; Fishing clubs of Japanese Americans; Golf clubs of Japanese Americans; Japanese American Citizens League; Neighborhood associations of Japanese Americans; Voluntary associations of Japanese Americans

Ethnic organizations of Jewish Americans, 102, 112

Ethnogenesis, defined, 101

European Americans: assimilation of, 83–84, 93–94, 101–2; citizenship of, 39; ethnicity of, 5, 33, 121, 122; intermarriage of, 99–100; Issei compared to, 33–35, 39; Nisei compared to, 41; reactions to, 34–35

Evacuation and internment of Japanese Americans: and American Civil Liberties Union, 47, 49; causes of, 81; characteristics of, 76; Clark on, 45; and collective organization, 42, 78–79, 133; and Communist party, 47–48; and Del E. Webb Company, 62; De Witt on, 45–46, 48, 60, 65; effects of, 61, 62–63, 69, 74–79, 92, 97, 151; and Executive Order 9066, 44, 60; exhibits about, 122; and Fair Play Committee, 67–68; and family structure, 62–63, 97, 151; of farm workers, 74, 92, 97; and FBI, 49; in Hawaii, 48–51; Hayakawa

Index

on, 79–80; Hearst newspapers on, 46; of Issei, 13, 62, 63, 70, 74–75, 97; and juvenile delinquency, 63; Knox on, 46, 48; La Guardia on, 47; Lippmann on, 47; and military forces, 49; Munson on, 45, 49; of Nisei, 13, 62, 63, 70, 75–76; and Public Proclamations 1 and 4, 60; Quakers on, 47; reactions to, 44–50, 62, 63, 64–74, 76–78, 81–82; of religious leaders, 64; F. Roosevelt on, 47, 48; and Sansei, 75, 76–78; and Santa Anita racetrack riot, 61; of small business owners, 74, 97; Stilwell on, 45; and urbanization, 92; and War Relocation Authority, 49, 62, 63, 69; Warren on, 46–47; and Wartime Civil Control Administration, 60. See also Discrimination against Japanese Americans

Evacuation Claims Act (1948), 74

Executive Order 9066, 44, 60

Factory workers in Japan, 11

Fair Play Committee (FPC), 67–68, 82

Family structure of Chinese Americans, 33

Family structure of Japanese Americans: and assimilation, 85, 97; changes in, 97–100; Chinese American family structure compared to, 33; collective organization of, 117; effects of, 33; and evacuation and internment, 62–63, 97, 151; and farm workers, 97; and primogeniture, 33; and small business owners, 33, 97; and World War I, 32–33. See also Intermarriage of Japanese Americans

Farm workers, Chinese American, 18, 21, 22. See also Chinese Americans

Farm workers, Filipino, 31

Farm workers, Japanese American: and alien land acts, 22–27; Bryan on, 23–24; in California, 19–27, 29, 39, 146; characteristics of, 22; Chinda on, 23; collective organization of, 19, 27, 39, 95; and Depression, 38; discrimination against, 38; education of, 19; and Estate of Tesubumi Yano case, 25; and ethnic economy, 29; ethnic hegemony of, 95, 149; evacuation and internment of, 74, 92, 97; and family structure, 97; and Filipino farm workers,

31; in Hawaii, 20, 21; and iemoto, 20; and Industrial Workers of the World, 21; interpersonal relationships of, 19; and Japanese Associations, 30; in labor unions, 20–21, 41, 95; and Mexican farm workers, 20, 30, 31; number of, 90, 92, 95, 146; origins of, 10–11, 15, 18; reactions to, 22–23, 29–32, 38, 46; strawberry production of, 149; success of, 39, 46; Webb on, 22–23; Wilson on, 23, 24. See also Contract laborers, Japanese American; Small business owners, Japanese American

Farm workers, Mexican, 20, 30, 31

FBI, 44, 45, 49

Feudalism, 6–8

Filipino Americans, 31, 50

Final Report (government document), 151

Finance, Japanese Americans in, 95

Fishermen, Japanese American, 74

Fishermen, Vietnamese American, 104, 128

Fishing clubs of Japanese Americans, 102

Fleming, Arthur S., 81

Flexible rigidities of Japanese Americans, 147

442nd Regimental Combat Team: heroism of, 66, 86, 89, 92; importance of, 92; motto of, 66; return from war of, 86; volunteers for, 50–51, 75, 81–82. See also Military forces

442nd Veterans Club, 86, 87

FPC, 67–68, 82

Fresno Rodo Domei Kai, 20, 21. See also Labor unions

Fukuoka prefecture, 15. See also Japan

Gaman, defined, 78

Gardena, California, 149

Gardeners Association, 31

Gentlemen's Agreement, 17, 24, 32, 39

"Glass ceiling," 131

"Go-betweens," 99

Goldberg, Arthur J., 81

Gold Rush, 17

Golf clubs of Japanese Americans, 102

Gompers, Samuel, 21

Greater East Asia Coprosperity Sphere, 43

Gromoff, Ishmael V., 81

Group vs. individual. See Collective organization of Japanese Americans

Hachiya (sergeant), 66
Harvard University, 130, 131
Hate crimes, 104, 128. See also Discrimination against Japanese Americans
Hawaii: annexation of, 17; Democratic party in, 87; economic structure of, 86, 87; martial law in, 48, 87; plantations in, 86, 87; Republican party in, 87; statehood of, 87–88; tourism in, 86, 87; white Americans in, 35
Hawaii, Japanese Americans in: and Buddhist temples, 50; characteristics of, 36; as contract laborers, 16, 20; evacuation and internment of, 48–51; as farm workers, 20, 21; Knox on, 48; in labor unions, 20, 21; and language schools, 50; in military forces, 75, 86; Munson on, 49; number of, 16, 35; political power of, 49–50, 86–87, 145, 152; F. Roosevelt on, 48; and statehood, 87–88
Hawaiian Provisional Battalion, 66, 75, 92
Hayakawa, S. I., 79–80
Hearst newspapers, 46
Heart Mountain Wyoming Center, 67–68, 82
Higher Wages Association, 20. See also Labor unions
Hiroshima prefecture, 15. See also Japan
Hokoku Seinen-dan, 72–73
Hong Kong, 127
Households. See Family structure of Japanese Americans
Hui, 27

Idaho, alien land acts in, 27
Ie. See Family structure of Japanese Americans
Iemoto, 7, 20, 28
Immigrants in United States, number of, 139
Immigration Exclusion Act (1924), 14, 18, 63–64
Immigration Reform Act (1965), 94
Imperial Rescript on Education, 4
Income of Chinese Americans, 144
Income of Japanese Americans, 1, 104, 144

Individualism, 105–6, 108, 115–16. See also Collective organization of Japanese Americans
Industrial Workers of the World (IWW), 21
Inheritance of Japanese Americans, 97–98. See also Family structure of Japanese Americans
Inouye, Daniel, 87, 132
Insurance careers, Japanese Americans in, 95
Intelligence work of Japanese Americans, 64–66
Intermarriage of European Americans, 99–100. See also Multiple ancestry
Intermarriage of Japanese Americans: amount of, 2, 84, 98, 99, 100, 118–19, 120, 125–26, 128; children of, 128–29; and ethnicity, 99, 125; of Issei, 98, 99; of Nisei, 99; of Sansei, 98, 99, 125. See also Family structure of Japanese Americans; Multiple ancestry
Internment. See Evacuation and internment of Japanese Americans
Interpersonal relationships of Japanese Americans: characteristics of, 107–10, 153; of contract laborers, 19; of farm workers, 19; of Nisei, 108–9; of Sansei, 109–10; and voluntary associations, 134. See also Collective organization of Japanese Americans
Inus, 72
Issei: characteristics of, 35; citizenship of, 87; collective organization of, 3, 5–6, 70, 91; defined, 2, 15; demoralization of, 62, 63, 74–75, 89, 97; education of, 94; and ethnic economy, 6; European Americans compared to, 33–35, 39; evacuation and internment of, 13, 62, 63, 70, 74–75, 97; and FBI, 44; homogeneity of, 3, 5–6; intermarriage of, 98, 99; in Japanese Associations, 113; and Nisei, 91–92, 97–98, 99; reactions to, 2; as small business owners, 93, 94; and sojourner mentality, 21; Speak English campaigns for, 50; and World War II, 43. See also Japanese Americans
IWW, 21

JACL. See Japanese American Citizens League

Index

JACP, 147

Jan Ken Po summer school, 116

Japan: and Cold War, 90–91; conscription law in, 11; constitution of, 4; economic growth of, 126–28; education in, 94; factory workers in, 11; imperialism of, 43; and Imperial Rescript on Education, 4; and Japanese American community, 34; and Japanese Americans, supervision of, 12, 13, 34; and Japanese Associations, 34, 43; land taxes in, 10–11; Meiji Restoration in, 10, 94; mine workers in, 11; open-door policy of, 10–12; and picture brides, 17–18; prefectures in, 15; and Russo-Japanese War, 12; and Satsuma Rebellion, 11; silk industry in, 11; and Sino-Japanese War, 11, 12; Tokugawa Shogunate in, 10

Japanese American Citizens League (JACL): collective organization of, 42; and discrimination, 113–14; and El Monte berry strike, 30; membership in, 102, 113; oratorical contest of, 32; origins of, 40, 42; purposes of, 40, 102; and redress movement, 79, 114; and Venice celery strike, 31

Japanese American Curriculum Project (JACP), 147. See also Asian American studies programs

Japanese American Library, 122

Japanese Americans: African Americans compared to, 35; characteristics of, 78, 104–5; Chinese Americans compared to, 16–18, 19; European Americans compared to, 33, 34, 35, 41; and Filipino Americans, 50; Japanese government supervision of, 12, 13, 34; Jewish Americans compared to, 122; number of, 17, 137; reactions to, 1–2, 35–36, 84; reasons for immigration of, 10–13, 15–16; time of immigration of, 14, 15, 17, 19, 137. See also Issei; Kibei; Nisei; Sansei; Yonsei; specific headings

Japanese Association of Los Angeles, 31

Japanese Associations: collective organization of, 42; and farm workers, 30; Issei in, 113; and Japanese government, 34, 43; origins of, 29–30, 42; purposes of, 30, 113. See also Central Japanese Association of Southern California

Japanese Farm Workers Union, 20. See also Labor unions

"Japanese in Agriculture" (oratorical contest), 32

Japanese Language School, 65–66, 68

Jewish Americans: assimilation of, 112; in colleges and universities, 130, 131; ethnic organizations of, 102, 112; Japanese Americans compared to, 122; and redress movement, 81

Juvenile delinquency of Japanese Americans, 63

Kansas, alien land acts in, 27

Kenjinkai, 34

Kibei, 45, 65, 66, 72. See also Japanese Americans

Knox, Frank, 46, 48

Korea, 127

"Kotonks," 36

Kumamoto prefecture, 15. See also Japan

Laborers Cooperative and Friendly Society, 31

Labor unions, Japanese Americans in, 20- 21, 41, 84, 95. See also specific labor unions

La Guardia, Fiorello, 47

Land taxes in Japan, 10–11

Language schools of Japanese Americans, 34, 50, 92, 115. See also San Francisco Oriental school

Lawyers, Japanese Americans as, 86, 87, 131–32. See also Employment of Japanese Americans

Lippmann, Walter, 47

Little Tokyo Businessman's Association, 31. See also Business and professional groups of Japanese Americans

Lordsburg Internment Camp, 68

Louisiana, alien land acts in, 27

"Loyalty" test, 69–72

Lungren, Daniel E., 81

McCarran-Walter Immigration Bill, 14, 87

MAGIC (diplomatic message code), 150

Manufacturing jobs of Chinese Americans, 18

Manzanar Relocation Center, 68
Marriage. See Arranged marriages of Japanese Americans; Intermarriage
Martial law in Hawaii, 48, 87
Marutani, William M., 81
Matsui, Robert, 132
Mechanical occupations of Chinese Americans, 18
Medal of Honor, 66
Meiji Restoration, 10, 94
Mexicans, as farm workers, 20, 30, 31
Midway, Battle of, 65
Midwest, Chinese Americans in, 138
Midwest, Japanese Americans in, 91, 138
Midwest, white Americans in, 138
Military Area No. 1, 60
Military forces, Japanese Americans in, 49, 65–67, 75, 86. See also 1800 Engineer Service Battalion; 442nd Regimental Combat Team; 100th Infantry Battalion
Military Intelligence Service Language School (MISLS), 65–66, 68
Military intelligence work of Japanese Americans, 64–66
Mineta, Norman, 132
Mine workers in Japan, 11
Minority success story of Japanese Americans, 2, 89–90. See also Stereotypes of Japanese Americans
MISLS, 65–66, 68
Mitchell, Hugh B., 81
Model minority, Japanese Americans as, 2, 89–90. See also Stereotypes of Japanese Americans
Montana, alien land acts in, 27
Multi-layered faith of Japanese Americans, 117
Multiple ancestry, 140. See also Intermarriage
Munson, Carl B., 45, 49
Mutual aid societies of Japanese Americans, 114–15, 135

National Association of Buddhist Ministries, 50. See also Buddhist temples
Nationality Act (1940), 73
National Japanese American Historical Society, 122
National Japanese American Museum, 122

Nativist movements in United States, 41
Navy. See Military forces
Nebraska, alien land acts in, 27
Neighborhood associations of Japanese Americans, 102
New Mexico, alien land acts in, 27
Newspapers. See Hearst newspapers; Vernacular newspapers of Japanese Americans
Nihonteki, 105
Nisei: assimilation of, 91–92; characteristics of, 35, 75–76, 79; collective organization of, 36–37; defined, 2, 15; discrimination against, 39, 103, 104; education of, 38–39; European Americans compared to, 41; evacuation and internment of, 13, 62, 63, 70, 75–76; intermarriage of, 99; interpersonal relationships of, 108–9; and Issei, 91–92, 97–98, 99; in language schools, 92, 115; in military forces, 65–67; military intelligence work of, 65, 66; reactions to, 2, 39; and redress movement, 80, 124; relativistic ethic of, 36–37, 93; and Sansei, 123; as small business owners, 93; as teachers, 39; and World War II, 43–44. See also Japanese Americans
Nisei Farmers League, 95, 114
"No-no's," 72
Northeast. See East Coast

100th Infantry Battalion, 66, 75, 92. See also Military forces
Open-door policy, 10–12
Oregon, alien land acts in, 27
Organizational momentum, 114, 135
Organization to Serve the Mother Country, 72–73
Oriental Exclusion Act (1924), 39

Pacific Rim, 126–28. See also Japan
Partnerships of Japanese Americans, 27
Pearl Harbor, 43–44
Perry, Matthew, 10
Persistent people, defined, 4
Personal Justice Denied (CWRIC), 81
Personal service work of Chinese Americans, 18
Picture brides, Japanese, 17–18
Plantations, 86, 87
Political machines, 5

Index

Political power of Japanese Americans: and assimilation, 132; and discrimination, 135; in Hawaii, 49–50, 86–87, 145, 152

Prefectural associations of Japanese Americans, 34

Primogeniture, 33

Professional services, Japanese Americans in, 95

Projects. See Evacuation and internment of Japanese Americans

Pseudo-kinship relationships of Japanese Americans, 7, 20, 28

Public administration, Japanese Americans in, 95

Public Proclamations 1 and 4, 60

Purple Heart Battalion, 66, 75, 92. See also Military forces

Quakers, 47

Quasi-kin relationships of Japanese Americans, 7, 20, 28

Railroad, transcontinental, 17

Rasmussen, Kai, 65

Reagan, Ronald, 81, 150

Real estate careers, Japanese Americans in, 95

Recreational organizations of Japanese Americans, 102, 115

Redress movement: and Commission on the Wartime Relocation and Incarceration of Citizens, 81; and ethnicity, 121, 124; and Japanese American Citizens League, 79, 114; and Jewish Americans, 81; and lawyers, 131–32; and Nisei, 80, 124; origins of, 79; reactions to, 79–82, 121; and Sansei, 80, 124, 131–32

"Red Scare" (1917), 21

Registration of Japanese Americans, 69–73. See also Evacuation and internment of Japanese Americans

Relativistic ethic of Japanese Americans: and assimilation, 9–10, 85; characteristics of, 8; and collective organization, 8, 9, 36, 93, 94, 116–17, 133; defined, 42, 93; effects of, 8, 36, 117; and ethnicity, 8–10; of Nisei, 36–37, 93; and religion, 9; of voluntary associations, 115, 136

Religion of Japanese Americans, 9, 64, 117. See also Buddhist temples

Relocation of Japanese Americans, 75, 85, 91, 92

Renunciants, Japanese American, 73–74

Reparations movement. See Redress movement

Report of Investigation on Arable Land (government document), 30

Report of the Investigation on Agricultural Land Outside the State (government document), 30

Republican party, 87

Reverse discrimination, 131. See also Discrimination against Japanese Americans

Riots of Japanese Americans, 61

Rodo Kyoyukai, 31

Roosevelt, Franklin D., 47, 48

Roosevelt, Theodore, 12, 13, 24

Rotating credit associations of Japanese Americans, 27–28, 149

Rural areas, Japanese Americans in, 18

Russo-Japanese War (1904–5), 12

San Francisco Bay Area, Japanese Americans in, 119–20. See also California, Japanese Americans in

San Francisco Oriental school, 24. See also Language schools of Japanese Americans

San Joaquin Valley growers' organization, 95

Sansei: characteristics of, 134; defined, 2, 15; discrimination against, 103, 104; and evacuation and internment, 75, 76–78; intermarriage of, 98, 99, 125; interpersonal relationships of, 109–10; isolation of, 110, 117; as lawyers, 131–32; and Nisei, 123; reactions to, 2, 103, 104; and redress movement, 80, 124, 131–32; in voluntary associations, 116, 125. See also Japanese Americans

Santa Anita racetrack riot, 61

Satsuma Rebellion, 11

Segregation of African Americans, 35, 83–84

Segregation of Japanese Americans: in California, 88; characteristics of, 35, 74, 83–84; in military forces, 66. See

also Discrimination against Japanese Americans
Shinto priests, 64
Shusin, defined, 115
Silk industry in Japan, 11
Singapore, 127
Sino-Japanese War (1894–95), 11, 12
Small business owners, Japanese American: and African Americans, 129–30; assimilation of, 85, 92–93; collective organization of, 38, 93; discrimination against, 38; and ethnic economy, 28–29; evacuation and internment of, 74, 97; and family structure, 33, 97; Issei as, 93, 94; Nisei as, 93; origins of, 38, 149; and primogeniture, 33; reactions to, 38; and tanomoshi, 149. See also Farm workers, Japanese American
Smithsonian Institution, 122
Social coercion, 113
Social memories of Japanese Americans, 110
Sojourner mentality of Japanese Americans, 11, 21
Sokuji Kikoku Hoshi-dan, 72–73
South, Chinese Americans in, 138
South, Japanese Americans in, 138
South, white Americans in, 138
Southern California Farm Federation, 31
Speak English campaigns, 50
Spontaneity of white Americans, 108–9
Stereotypes of Japanese Americans, 111, 129. See also Model minority
Stilwell, Joseph, 45
Stockton, California murders, 104
Strawberry production of Japanese Americans, 149
Strikes of Japanese Americans, 20, 30–31
Structural assimilation, defined, 83. See also Assimilation
Structural constraints of Japanese Americans, 2–3, 103, 132
Sugar Beet and Farm Laborers' Union of Oxnard, 20, 21. See also Labor unions
Sugar plantations, 86, 87

Taiwan, 127
Tanomoshi, 27–28, 149
Teachers, Japanese Americans as, 39, 85–86. See also Employment of Japanese Americans

Terrorism against Japanese Americans, 91. See also Discrimination against Japanese Americans
Texas, alien land acts in, 27
Tokugawa Shogunate, 10
Tourism in Hawaii, 86, 87
Toyota bashing parties, 127. See also Discrimination against Japanese Americans
Trade, Japanese Americans in, 95
Transcontinental railroad, 17
Truman, Harry, 68, 73
Tule Lake camp, 67, 71–73

UCLA, 130
Universities, Japanese Americans in, 130–31
Universities, Jewish Americans in, 130, 131
University of California at Los Angeles (UCLA), 130
Urbanization of Chinese Americans, 18
Urbanization of Japanese Americans, 92

Venice celery strike, 20, 31
Vernacular newspapers of Japanese Americans, 43, 44
Vertically integrated ethnic economy, defined, 29. See also Ethnic economy of Japanese Americans
Vietnamese Americans, 104, 128, 129
Voluntary associations of Japanese Americans: and alien land laws, 113; collective organization of, 113, 133, 153; and discrimination, 134–35; and interpersonal relationships, 134; membership in, 102–3, 124–25; organizational momentum of, 114, 135; origins of, 8, 9–10; purposes of, 113, 115, 131, 135; relativistic ethic of, 115, 136; Sansei in, 116, 125; social coercion in, 113

Wakayama prefecture, 15. See also Japan
War Relocation Authority (WRA): and assimilation, 75, 85, 91, 92; and evacuation and internment, 49, 62, 63, 69; and Hokoku Seinen-dan, 72–73; and registration, 72–73; and relocation, 75, 85, 91, 92; and Sokuji Kikoku Hoshi-dan, 72–73; and urbanization, 92

Index

Warren, Earl, 46–47
Wartime Civil Control Administration (WCCA), 60
Washington (state), alien land acts in, 27
WCCA, 60
Webb, U. S., 22–23
West Coast, Chinese Americans on, 18, 119–20, 138
West Coast, Japanese Americans on, 18, 35–36, 85, 138. See also California, Japanese Americans in
West Coast, white Americans on, 138
White Americans: on East Coast, 138; education of, 144; in Hawaii, 35; in Midwest, 138; number of, 137; in South, 138; spontaneity of, 108–9; on West Coast, 138
Willoughby, Charles, 64–65
Wilson, Willie, 130
Wilson, Woodrow, 23, 24
World War I, 32–33
World War II, 43–44
WRA. See War Relocation Authority

Yamaguchi prefecture, 15. See also Japan
"Yes-yes's," 72
Yonsei, defined, 116. See also Japanese Americans
Young Men's Organization to Serve the Mother Country, 72–73

DAVID J. O'BRIEN is Professor in the departments of Rural Sociology and Community Development at the University of Missouri-Columbia.

STEPHEN S. FUGITA is Associate Professor of Psychology and Ethnic Studies at Santa Clara University.

They are coauthors of *Japanese Americans: The Persistence of Community* (University of Washington Press, 1991).